# THE HEALTH OF THE VIOLIN

## AND THE VIOLA AND CELLO

*Practical Advice on the Acquisition,
Maintenance, Adjustment, and
Conservation of Bowed Instruments*

By Lucien Greilsamer

Translated by Henry A. Strobel
From the Original French:

L'HYGIÈNE DU VIOLON
de l'Alto et du Violoncelle

*CONSEILS PRATIQUES SUR L'ACQUISITION
L'ENTRETIEN, LE RÈGLAGE, LA CONSER-
VATION DES INSTRUMENTS À ARCHET*

*Second Edition*

Published by Henry Strobel, Violin Maker & Publisher
10878 Mill Creek Road
Aumsville, Oregon
97325

www.HenryStrobel.com

Library of Congress Catalog
Card Number:
91-67787

ISBN 0-9620673-4-2

First Edition November 1991
Second Printing March 1993
Second Edition October 1994
Second Printing of the Second Edition. December 1996
Third Printing of the Second Edition. September 1999
Fourth Printing of the Second Edition 2002
Fifth Printing of the Second Edition, November 2006

Printed in the United States of America

See the back cover for other books in the
Strobel Series for Violin Makers

4

## PREFACE TO THE FIRST AMERICAN EDITION

Several months ago I chanced to find the original of this book. It seemed to me full of good sense and insight. It remains substantially valid, although the specifics of, say, string manufacture, have advanced since 1910. As far as I know, it has never before been available in English.

This is the third book in my series for violin makers and those with related interests. Unlike the others, this is *not* a reference book, but a background book to *read* for pleasure and knowledge, and a book to *have* as an unusual - and unusually good - example of the literature of the violin maker and violinist. Whether you agree with him on particular points is up to you. In most cases I do. The best reasons for reading it, apart from its sound information, are its *perspective* and direct, pithy, even earthy, manner. Vannes' *Dictionnaire Universel des Luthiers* says he was an "Alsatian writer (*musicographe alsacien*), an author of very interesting works on lutherie."

For utility and economy the format here is similar to the previous books, although I have used typefaces and a column width more reminiscent of the original. The original has 121 smaller pages followed by a table of contents (now moved to the front). This is M. Greilsamer's book, not mine (except for translation errors). Any editorial comments I have added are within brackets, as [ . . . ].

The illustrations and plates have been reproduced full size. The plates have been renumbered for a more logical placement within the text.

I confess I am not a speaker or student of French, so this translation became a challenge and perhaps a modest personal *tour de force*. It has given me welcome breaks from the boredom of bridge fitting, although I could spare relatively little time for it. My bookshelf happened to hold a venerable leather bound *Spiers and Surennes's FRENCH AND ENGLISH Pronouncing Dictionary* of 1898, which has surprisingly survived my countless consultations. I trust you will find the translation, if imperfect, at least useful, and retaining some of M. Greilsamer's Gallic flavor.

I have appreciated his wit and wisdom and wish you the same.

Henry Strobel
November, 1991

Lucien Greilsamer

———

# THE "HEALTH" OF THE VIOLIN

[CONDITION AND CARE OF THE VIOLIN]

AND OF THE VIOLA AND CELLO

———

*PRACTICAL ADVICE ON THE ACQUISITION, MAINTENANCE, ADJUSTMENT, AND CONSERVATION OF BOWED INSTRUMENTS*

———

With 50 Explanatory Figures and 4 Plates
[Some of the figures are not numbered; these are within the composite plates.]

Present Publisher's Notice:

This is a copyrighted, new, original, annotated translation of a work in French, the copyright of which has expired, and which was originally published by:

## PARIS
LIBRAIRIE CH. DELAGRAVE
15, RUE SOUFFLOT, 15

[The publisher of the original French language edition in 1910.]

## TABLE OF CONTENTS

# CHAPTER I

## GENERAL "HEALTH": CONDITIONS IN WHICH AN INSTRUMENT SHOULD BE KEPT TO MAINTAIN ITS GOOD QUALITIES.

Simple folk and poets say the violin has a soul. Virtuoso violinists don't think so; they'd rather not share their glory, and if they don't mind admitting to a soul greater than that of other men, when it's a question of violins, they apply this word only to that stick of wood connecting the table and back. And knowing that this moveable organ regulates the whole structure of the sound they abuse it by frequent, often fruitless, movements. [Âme means soul or sound post.]

Yet, as enamored as they are with their own personality, these artists see in their bound companion something more than a tool like a piano, cornet, or clarinet. The setting it apart from and above the multitude of other instruments, it was suggested, they attribute, as an aesthetic complement to its acoustic qualities, to the beautiful dégradé [wear or patina] that forms from the charming play of light on the varnish of the back, and from the wear on the back of the scroll.

It may be that violins were always hung up on the wall, which is, all things considered, nothing more ridiculous than hanging up the dinner plates, but that was never an ordinary practice.

The fine cases of the 17th and 18th centuries, bound with tooled leather and gold leaf, decorated with incised clasps, gilded in bronze or in silver, lushly upholstered inside in Venetian silk velour, just as the lighter, more portable, less rich (for the use of professional musicians, also less rich), which have come down to us, are the evidence.

The latter, infinitely more numerous, explain the reason for the *wear* which is so highly valued, and for those unexplained and picturesque scrapes that every respectable old violin must bear with honor. Cases for carrying violins in town were relatively light and practical, but the instruments were poorly housed. Generally unpadded inside, they did not match the violin's shape; one tied the head at the front, then the bow at it's side. The poorly kept instrument sustained a series of abrasions against the walls of the case at every movement of the traveler, and enroute there took place the first battle between fiddle and bow, in anticipation of that to come in the concert hall.

Thus was produced in part the beauteous *wear* that produces the admiration of the connoisseur. The rest is the result of other causes, as we all know.

One may add that the old French and German violins were shaken about just as their Italian counterparts; you could hardly tell a logical person that different nationalities treated them differently.

Other abrasions too resulted in this *wear* and have given it its final patina.

For the cello, the places where wear is noticed are easily explained from contact with the legs and by the motion of the left hand; it's not the same for the violin.

What caused the large triangle that covers almost the entire back on the old Italian instruments? And those bald spots on the table right and left of the tailpiece, and lastly what abuse often resulted in extreme wear to the wood on the right side of the scroll?

For the key to this little enigma, we need only go back a little into the past.

In Italy, a great many violinists habitually played with the instrument flat against the chest, as we moderns "pipe". This completes the triangle that began in the case. As for the wear on the table to the right of the tailpiece, we should know that up till the beginning of the 19th century, there was no rule for holding the instrument. Some held their chin on the right side of the table, others on the tailpiece, and finally others, as is our practice nowadays, on the left side. The chin rest was not yet invented (it dates from Spohr), and the chin quickly marked its place on the tender skin of the Italian varnish.

I might add that the cut of the clothing was quite unsuitable for holding the instrument. Indeed, the violinists of the time would have cried "miracle" had they seen our modern virtuosos tuning with the left hand during pauses and rests, keeping their violin in its position, and they would not have believed their eyes had they witnessed a little tour de force unknown to Paganini, which consists in letting go the violin completely to hold the bow or to turn the page for the pianist, and to hold that violin in its horizontal position solely with the pressure of the chin. The cut of our modern clothing along with the help of a good chin rest and a round cushion placed under the clothing are enough to work this miracle.

But how did our ancestors tune? They held the scroll of their violin against a piece of furniture, a desk, or the back of a chair, and by this means, obsolete but sure, they were able to adjust the two left pegs. I have seen a superb Amati, in an otherwise well preserved condition, whose head was literally worn away on the right side as a consequence of this practice.

We still need to know whether it is best for a violin to be hung on the wall, put in a display case, or sealed up in a case. (Of course it is understood, unless indicated otherwise, that everything we have to say in the case of the violin applies equally to the viola and cello.)

Perhaps you have hung your violin on a wall to decorate your apartment? Was it to enjoy the view of a favorite antique? To have it ready to hand without the slight annoyance of unpacking it from an awkward case or, in fact, to preserve, if not improve, your violin's good qualities? You must have noticed that, regardless of its nature or origin, it always behaved in the following way: at first it rapidly went out of tune to a very noticeable degree, then, within a short time, the strings snapped one after the other in the following order, E, A, G, D. This last string, which never breaks on instruments provided with cases and has to be changed when worn out from playing, is the one which finally breaks in its turn.

But from time to time you wanted to play an instrument, and found that it had become rough and stubborn, that the fourth string sounded like scrap iron, that the others stayed poorly in tune, and that, in short, it had changed for the worse. It was necessary to handle it for a while, to do some scales, to play a certain number of bow strokes, and to warm it up, as we say in the terms of the trade, to restore its fluid timbre and ease of playing.

This experience then has shown you that there is nothing more disastrous for string instruments than to be thus exposed, however the location is arranged. Nor are the more comfortable living quarters, where the heat is controlled in the winter, where ventilation is provided year round, free from blame; the main reason is that houses with furnaces and humid locations become real disasters, as we shall see. During the long months of winter, in the presence of artificial heat, the air becomes dry, it dries out the strings, making them fragile, the metal winding of the fourth string separates from the gut, and produces the steely clatter we have just mentioned; this extremely dry air dries out the wood too, and gives it a tendency to a hoarse and veiled sound. Then when the apartment is aired out, under the abrupt invasion of the cold air, the wood, varnish, glue, and all suddenly shrink, to resume at once, in one jump, the extremes of swelling and drying. The brutal passage therefore from hot to cold, and vice versa, cannot but leave the instruments rebellious to the bow.

Let's assume now a humid but unheated place. Then the situation grows more serious. As the humidity softens the glue, little by little the neck, under the attraction of the strings, goes down in front, the fingerboard approaches the table, the bridge appears too high and the violin becomes unplayable. Likewise it happens that the neck may end up completely separated from the button to which it had been glued.

Although the summer may be less injurious, the contrast between the sultry days and the cool nights, the sudden storms, in short the changing scene of the weather; these are all bad for the health of the violin.

These difficulties can be avoided by keeping the violin in a suitably constructed case. When you take out your violin, if it is healthy and well made, then although you have not touched it for fifteen days, it will be nearly in tune, and little if anything will be needed to get it ready to play. The chanterelle only may have sharpened; this happens generally whenever there are large changes in barometric pressure. Thus enclosed, the instrument has been subjected to a minimum of foreign influences.

What is the best case?

First of all one whose outside is of varnished wood or covered with leather. This is the best insulator. Beware of cases made of metal and covered with Morocco leather.

Metal always draws moisture. As for the inside, it should be furnished with a soft fabric. Wool is fine for instruments that are handled daily. But for those that are not played regularly or that are considered as objects in a collection, velour or cotton plush, or preferably silk plush, are best, for these materials are resistant to the moths that are so hungry for wool.

In recent years the old so-called French cases were abandoned in favor of the "elegant" shaped cases, easier to carry. If you have a valuable instrument, don't give up anything for a false elegance and don't be afraid to put it into a case strong enough to withstand bumps, and thick enough to protect it from inclement weather.

Very few people hang vastly valuable Cremonas on their wall, and most amateurs or collectors place them in display cases as the museums do.

It is easy to conclude from what we are about to learn that, although a glass display case protects instruments to some extent, it is not the equivalent of an efficient regular case. The glass case, moreover, is to blame for a fault peculiar to it, that is, color fading.

We have in fact observed that exposure to light wastes the lovely color of the old Italian varnish. The loss of color is general when the instruments are exposed to light on all sides. Thus it has happened that certain Cremonas that had passed for deeply colored a little over fifty years ago, we now know to be of a very faded tint. The fading is partial when only one of the two faces receives the light. Some authors, short on facts, wrote on this subject that some of the old master Luthiers had a habit of varnishing the table or back of their instruments a lighter color than the rest.

Such an assemblage of facts now leads us to consider the logic of the practices that I have seen violinists try and which of them are worth following.

One ought not play in a salon or in a concert hall without having given the instrument time to adapt to the ambient temperature; failing this the performer will be obliged to correct the tuning of his violin throughout his piece. We know how unpleasant tuning variation is to the listener and how prejudicial it is to the artist who is no longer the master of his medium, preoccupied as he is with the need to watch for pauses and rests to chance a twist at his peg. One practice, aimed at saving the chanterelle, consists in lowering it when the violin is put back into the case after playing. I have noted that this does not prevent this string from breaking if it is predestined to an early end, which usually happens when it is first tightened. This habit once again upsets the equilibrium of the instrument.

Do you want a violin to be playable? It must keep the steadiest possible tuning. Thanks to the force of its strings, an instrument keeps that equilibrium that assures its stability of tuning and exhibits at the same time those tonal qualities with which it is endowed. This formidable string force, which some consider the great ravager of bowed instruments, is indeed what provides their vibratory energy, without which the sound would have neither volume nor beauty.

A violin that has been unplayed for a long time, and lays unstrung, when fitted up again, even with the same strings, does not stay in tune, and for some time remains inferior from the viewpoint of tone.

I mention an appropriate story that came from Sivori. Called to perform in a concert at Genoa, (I don't know the details), the city authorities requested him to play on Paganini's violin, which was religiously kept in a glass display case in the museum, and which no one had touched for years. The day of the concert, Sivori carefully picked up the Guarnerius, which he intended to use then for the recital. He immediately found he could get nothing good out of it; the famous violin would not stay in tune and its tone was atrocious. He said nothing, but in the concert that evening he performed on his own instrument with great success, which added to the illusion of hearing anew the resounding "Cannon" of Paganini, under the fingers of his sole and celebrated student.

When you come to use a violin that has not been played in a long time, you may be rather disappointed, observing that it has lost its good qualities. This inferiority is transitory; fitted up and played for a while, it becomes again what it was before, usually in a fairly short time, which can range from fifteen days to a month. It frequently happens that the possessor of a beautiful violin, ignorant of this fact, imagines that it needs repair and takes it to the luthier. We need not add that if the luthier is intelligent he will not touch it, unless he sees a physical defect. [The perennial question, how much does the violin itself adapt and how much does the player adapt to it is not easy to answer objectively. There is some of each.]

The breaking of a string is enough to upset the equilibrium of an instrument, and it is only some minutes after the broken string has been replaced that the previous equilibrium is regained.

These phenomena have given birth to a widespread prejudice that a violin loses its good qualities if it is not played, and that, on the other hand, it acquires new virtues from continuous use. So we often see owners of splendid Cremonas asking students, or even artists, the favor of playing them. The fools! Apart from the accidents to which violins are more or less predestined, especially in careless or awkward hands, we can testify that a Cremona does not gain, on the contrary, it loses from being played, especially when it becomes the war horse of a professional artist who literally uses it up.

The old instruments reached their peak a long time ago, and nearly all are declining rather than improving. But it is prodigious that they have lived so long, and the longevity of these Methusalahs that have seen come and go so many generations of instrumental singers, beaters, scrapers, or whistlers is not the least of their marvelous unique characteristics.

But you see why great toned Italian instruments have become more and more rare, and are sought by virtuosos who seek to be heard in our great concert halls.

What I have said about old instruments also applies to some extent to new ones, provided that they are very good. A new instrument needs to be played for some time, not because playing procures its good qualities, but because they are daily handled, and constantly kept in tune, at the tension necessary to place all their parts in equilibrium.

Beyond this point the violin will not improve further. I believe that instruments of the old Italian makers were therefore as good, if not better, than they are today, in the first years after they were built.

You owners of good violins, be careful if you let them be played, and remember how the famous collector Labitte shrewdly expressed this when he said, not uncourageously, "the virtuosos are the great enemies of violins".

Finally, de la Palisse added:
"Would you like a preventive, sure way to preserve your violins? Don't lend them to anyone."

At the beginning of this chapter, I talked a lot about humidity and its ill effects. To finish off this subject, a final bit of advice: Don't be in a hurry to shut up your violin in its case after using it. First set it on a piece of furniture for a few minutes - any kind except a chair, which might be chosen by someone nearsighted or distracted.

Why do this? - While performing your spirit is immersed in the ideal, then settling down to terra firma, you expound on the diverse inspirations of the renowned masters, or maybe of your own and, without being aware of it, your breath condenses prosaically on the table of your violin in a vapor deadly for the varnish and enters it through the f-holes. If you prevent this humidity from evaporating by immediately enclosing the violin in its case every time you stop playing, it will eventually soak the wood fibers, and soften them to the point of completely spoiling the instrument. To your great concern you will see it worsen day by day, stricken with a debility of whose cause you haven't a clue.

—————

# CHAPTER II

## THE STRINGS: THEORY OF FITTING UP; TABLE OF PRACTICAL OPTIMUM GAUGES

The virtuoso, a skilled player and good musician, is meticulous about the adjustment of his instrument. It doesn't take much to alter the beauty of its voice, to make good intonation difficult, and to compromise the outcome of the best efforts. If he is less sure of his instrument than himself, he loses the confidence that is essential to artistic execution.

The layman doubtless thinks that once all the parts needed to make a violin have been assembled, the finished violin is ready to play.

Those things that by virtue of their position, nature, and proportions give the sound box its musical vitality, since they most of all contribute precisely to the equilibrium without which no beauty of sound is possible, are: the strings, the bridge, the post and the bar, depending on the *stop* and the *fingerboard projection*.

If amateurs are sometimes annoyed that the factory delivers poor quality strings, the violins, in turn, would often be right to complain that their owners overburden them in a way that is incompatible with their nature; such a spirited horse has a tender mouth that is curbed with too strong a bit.

To properly understand string adjustment, we need to first know what the average gauge should be, and how this diameter may vary from one string to another.

From the day that lutherie first became a rational and precise art, Luthiers no doubt were concerned with finding a practical method of selecting strings, which had become an arbitrary matter of trial and error, and their search was to be singularly facilitated by the discoveries of their contemporary Mersenne (1588-1648), who set down the laws of the vibration of strings, laws which were explained theoretically in 1716 by the English mathematician Taylor.

Here is the problem before us:

If we take as a basis the chanterelle, and we give it a diameter of half a millimeter, that is to say the minimum that theoretical and experimental acoustics allows for a 33 centimeter long gut string:

1. In what ratio to this should we set the diameter of the other strings?
2. Should we give them less, the same, or greater tension?

Beginning experimentally, we reason as follows.
We set up our violin with four strings of equal diameter (taking for a standard the E), and tune it in fifths as usual: we note that the A is under much less tension than the E, the D less than the A, and the G less than the D. We pass the bow over the instrument: we observe that the tension is far too weak to make the instrument vibrate with the required energy; the sound is poor, small, and thin, with no carrying power and a bad quality. I say bad quality, for although with its tension, the E string, in this case, is the only one able to produce a suitable sound, it is not the same for the others, experience having shown that the sound of a stretched string is the more beautiful the nearer it is to the breaking point. It has been calculated that the tension of the strings of a well adjusted instrument is never less than a fifth of that which would cause them to break.

The chanterelle exceeds this measure, and the tension of this string, high relative to the others, is not by chance. It is based on the structure of the instrument which demands that the right foot of the bridge be loaded much more than the left.

Here are the exact figures for the violin:

|   | TENSION | RESISTANCE [breaking] |
|---|---------|----------------------|
| E | 8.965 kg | 14.4 kg |
| A | 6.875 kg | 18.5 kg |
| D | 6.327 kg | 29.3 kg |
| G | 6.255 kg | 22.3 kg |

Going back to our violin fitted with four strings of equal diameter: In observing that the tension of the strings is more or less weak beginning from the E, and ending with the G, we have simply experienced in part a law of Mersenne:

*The vibration numbers of strings are in direct proportion to the square root of the force with which they are stretched.*

["vibration numbers" means the *frequency* or vibrations per second, which we nowadays term *Herz*.]

As the tension of the strings, except the E, is insufficient to make our instrument vibrate vigorously, we are going to choose larger diameters, taking advantage of another law of Mersenne:

*The vibration number of strings of the same density is in inverse proportion to their diameter.*

We learn now, by expressing this law, the ratio in which we must select the other three strings.

In effect, let's assume two strings of steel of the same length, one with a diameter double that of the other. The narrower would produce a number of vibrations twice as great, and the other would thus sound an octave lower. Now let's set the relationship of the diameters as two to three; the narrower will produce three vibrations while the wider will produce only two and, with equal tension, will sound a fifth, of course.

This is just what we're looking for, since we want to tune our violin in fifths, and the ratio of diameters will have to be three to two.

Keeping the diameter of half a millimeter for the chanterelle we get the following series:

E: 1/2 or 8/16 A: 12/16 D: 18/16 G: 27/16

Now let's try to fit up the violin according to these conditions: we will find three strings satisfactory and the fourth, the G, bad. Its diameter will be too great relative to its length; we will find intonation difficult and practically impossible with a short section of string.

We have to get through this business, and providentially there is one more law of Mersenne that's going to settle it:

*The vibration numbers of strings are in inverse proportion to the square roots of the densities.*

The problem is solved: we wind a very thin wire around a narrow string, for example a chanterelle, which will also serve to give this string the total desired diameter, according to the metal used, the diameter of the gut and that of the wire.

You now see why, we may say in passing, strings wound with copper should be wider than those wound with silver, the density of this metal being greater than that of copper.

We can then, by selecting the diameter of the *spun string*, as it is called, provide the instrument with a fourth string narrow enough to allow shifting to all positions, yet offering the necessary and adequate tension.

What we do for the violin, we can repeat for the viola and cello, and we will see that there is an even greater need for wound strings on those two instruments. We note also that the low strings, the C of the viola and of the cello, can tolerate a diameter proportionately larger than the fourth string of the violin. This is justified by the structure itself of these two instruments and does not present any real inconvenience, since the high positions are not used on these strings in playing the viola or the cello, as far as orchestra instruments are concerned. For a solo, it's another matter. Cello virtuosos have always complained about their C, and the difficulties of intonation that trouble this string find their cause in its excessive diameter. You can be sure there is no simple remedy and we are presented with a big problem.

Suppose that we diminish the diameter of the gut but not that of the wire: the composite density of the string will be insufficient. Now if we increase the diameter of the wire the string will become too stiff, and we will not have improved anything.

I do know a cure, but it reminds me too much of a consultation given by a young doctor I know, to whom there came one day a poor devil of a laborer, completely worn out by work, anemic to his marrow, and on top of everything else having to feed a large family.:

"My friend," the conscientious disciple of Asclepius [Greek god of healing] said to him, "your case is serious. Eat a good steak, drink some Bordeaux, and go rest a few months in the country."

That doctor was not very wise, but he was certainly truthful.

There is in fact only one cure for the illness I pointed out above, and it's not within the reach of everyone.

It consists in decreasing the diameter of the gut and, by means of a sufficiently flexible and not too thick wire, obtaining the total density necessary for a good tone.

It's nothing more than a question of finding a metal whose density is higher than that of silver: platinum answers our need admirably and it has one other good quality, its flexibility. Gold, strictly speaking, could replace it... I was going to say .... for the poor.

If we proceed from the domain of theory to the practical, we learn that we can't slavishly calculate ideal strings isolated from all outside influence. In an instrument, we must take into account the density of the wood, its elasticity, its thickness, the air volume of the box, the height and shape of the archings, the tension of the bar, and of course the post. These elements, according to their role, must modify in some measure the progression of string diameters, and as they are never exactly the same from one instrument to another, it isn't possible to set a fixed rule. Touch and hearing are the only guides. You can reason beforehand according to the customer and the temperament of his instrument, but only by feeling your way will you arrive at the exact point. Having done this, you need only measure the diameter of the strings with a caliper, preferably a Palmer friction type in hundredths [of millimeters], and then stick with these dimensions in the future.

Average measures have been given which are much too variable to be useful.

I will point out those that seem best to me, including:

|  | Appian-Bennewitz: | | | |
|--------|--------|--------|--------|--------|
| Violin | E 65 | A 85 | D 110 | G 90 |
| Viola | A 80 | D 100 | G 85 | C 120 |
| Cello | A 125 | D 160 | G 160 | C 220 |

|  | Tolbecque: | | | |
|--------|--------|--------|--------|--------|
| Violin | E 60 | A 80 | D 115 | G 90 |
| Viola | A 85 | D 115 | G 85 | C 120 |
| Cello | A 120 | D 140 | G 125 | C 187 |

For the violin, I have seen used, by my teachers and by other great artists, measures that I consider to be well suited for examples of the best period of Stradivarius and for comparable models of Guarnerius such as these dimensions:

Violin E: 58-60 A: 78-80 D: 105-110 G: silver 85

All the above measures are in hundredths of millimeters.

You will notice that the diameter of the G that I have shown corresponds to a string overspun with silver. It would have to be much greater for one spun with copper.

It happens that some instruments require a little more force on the part of the strings. In this case attention must be placed on the D. This is the string that I consider as foremost in achieving definitively the regulation of the violin.

The manufacture of strings from the intestines of sheep developed at the same time as the art of violin making, and Italy enjoyed this double monopoly for a long time.

Much later, after that country had managed to lose the secret of bowed instruments, it nevertheless continued to benefit from its unquestioned reputation as a producer of strings, and still in our day people ask for Neapolitan strings, to the point that almost all the odd strings of Italy go under that designation.

The superiority of strings of animal origin, and the reasons that those from Italy were the best, were already known at the time of Nicolo Amati. A passage from the work of Mersenne on music is our witness.

Indeed, we have a hundred years later greatly perfected the method of adjusting instruments, but already toward the middle of the 18th century, the ever increasing demands of the art of the violin that was taking its flight with Corelli, inspired an extraordinary man, the famed *string maker* Angelo Angelucci, to whom we owe the last refinements of this industry without which "the lyre is mute."

The truth and durability of strings have always been the nightmare of violinists; it appears that on both counts the strings of Angelo Angelucci left little to be desired.

The method pointed out by Le Roy in his work on the lute which appeared in 1570, to check whether a string is true, is still the only one we know: it consists in taking the string at its two ends between the thumb and the index finger of each hand, stretching it moderately and placing it in vibration with the little finger. If you see distinctly the outline of two strings, it is true, otherwise, it is false. This procedure gives worthwhile results, especially for fine strings such as chanterelles. [Such a crude check is pointless with modern high quality strings.]

The only really effective test is, after the violin has been fitted up and kept in tune for a time, to verify whether all the fifths between two adjacent strings are found exactly opposite each other. In this case, the strings are perfectly cylindrical, and the diameter is equal throughout their whole length.

How do you recognize the quality of a string? - Only by playing it. An entire lot can be bad, just as a whole batch of bread can be scorched in the oven, or kneaded with spoiled flour. There are some outward signs that allow us to guess, but they are not very trustworthy.

Chanterelles should be transparent, and after squeezing a bundle in the hand, they should appear elastic and return immediately like a steel spring, without cracking. They should not change color when compressed. These indications confirm that the stiffness was not obtained artificially with aluminum salts.

The A and D strings on the contrary should be very soft when compressed, but they should promptly return to their cylindrical state without cracking. If they were too hard intonation would be difficult, and the quality of the sound bad.

In general, strings that have a lot of twist are more flexible, more elastic than others. The are best from the viewpoint of tone and, what is not to be disdained, stability.

As for the wound strings that need to have been stretched at a certain level of humidity before being covered with the wire called *cannetille* (wire ribbon) to properly incorporate it with the gut, only experience can fairly judge.

There are violinists who from time to time lightly oil their strings while they are on the instrument, intending to protect them from humidity. I will not advise following their example since the oil has the disadvantage of greasing the bow and removing its bite.

I will not say more than a note about steel chanterelles. They are a faulty product that cuts the pegs, the nut, the bridge, the tailpiece and the fingers of the performer; they quickly wear out the hair of the bow. As for their tone quality, I leave to my readers the task of appraising it according to the sensitivity of their ears. [Times, tastes, and strings have changed.]

———————

# CHAPTER III

## THE STOP: DIFFERENT METHODS OF DETERMINING AND CHECKING IT. TABLE OF OPTIMUM MEASUREMENTS

The length of the vibrating portion of the strings on bowed instruments is not arbitrary, and the care that the old Luthiers of Italy took in indicating by the inside nicks of the f-holes the exact position of the bridge shows what importance they assigned to this measurement. I will pass over the purpose of this task while trying find out how they established the string length from the nut to the bridge, to which the name *diapason* (stop) has been given. It can be said, in general, that it is somewhat less than the overall length of the box of the instrument. For the violin, for example, if we allow that the distance from the nut to the inside nicks of the f-holes is 32.5 centimeters, the length of the string in round numbers will be 33 centimeters.

Up until the present, these reasons were not formulated, and when a expert seriously tells you how to determine or to correct the stop, he knows theoretically no more than you, but he knows the proportion on which the stop is in fact set, and the measures which we have more or less agreed to adopt.

Without going to the heart of the question, it is useful to be aware that the ancients understood the stop differently than we do. Today, the measure of the stop is uniform, whoever may be the owner of the instrument. With the ancients, this measure varied with the dimensions of the box, so that a small instrument could hardly be played with a large hand. We presume that these were specifically destined for delicate hands, woman's, most likely, otherwise we could not explain their existence.

The writings of the time elsewhere teach us that in 18th century Italy young ladies were addicted, in large part, to studying bowed instruments, and that they formed, especially in certain religious communities, respected symphonies.

We can easily satisfy ourselves then why Italy has left us such a large number of instruments of small pattern, and we understand so much better why, for some years, we have seen our concert halls invaded by a charming lot of [feminine] violinists, violists, cellists, and even bassists, whether as soloists or in the orchestra. I most cordially applaud this conquest, an echo of a distant time, and I hope that, following my advice, violins, basses, violas, and cellos will become docile and submissive slaves in these slender and delicate hands.

Nowadays, no matter who the player is, if the distance indicated by the notches of the f-holes of an old instrument appears to be too short, the instrument is said to have a wrong stop, and the bridge is moved in accordance with the new law. It's fortunate that they don't move the f-holes themselves. On the other hand, when the neck lacks the regulation dimension, it's the last thing corrected.

In the time of Stradivarius, the neck of the violin was short by two *lignes* [4.5 mm], and it is to Viotti that we owe the present dimension, which is required for modern technique.

There's an objection here. If everything was calculated with such precision in the work of the old masters, how is it that lengthening the stop did not destroy the overall equilibrium of the instrument, but on the contrary improved it?

It's easy to find the explanation for this apparent contradiction. The old instruments didn't originally sound better or worse than today: they sounded different. The *A* was considerably lower, the strings were under less tension, and the different sound had more sweetness and less carrying power. But with the modern *renversement* [fingerboard projection], necessitated by the progressive raising of the *A*, the equilibrium was changed. Then, to resist the greater tension of the strings, the length and height of the bar was increased; with these conditions, the lengthening of the stop could only enhance the vibration, which would have been very short, very dry, had the old string length been kept.

This leads us naturally to what is called the *fingerboard projection,* and the study of it will allow us to determine in practice the height of the strings over the fingerboard, and the angle that they ought to have over the bridge.

First, I am going to point out how the stop is calculated and the exact measurements that result from different ways of doing this.

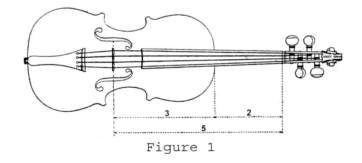

Figure 1

There are two ways of establishing the stop:

1. Divide the distance from the nut to the inside notches of the f-holes into five parts, two for the neck (from the nut to the edge of the table), and three for the table (from the edge of the table to the inside notches of the f-holes). Fig. 1.

2. Divide this distance into a dozen parts, five for the neck (from the nut to the purfling or to the rib), and seven for the table (from the purfling or the rib to the inside notches of the f-holes).

Here is an example of the stop calculated in the first way:

Distance from the nut to the notches of the f-holes:

| Violin | Viola | Cello |
|--------|-------|-------|
| 32.5 cm | 36.5 cm | 69.5 cm |

Distance from the edge of the table to the notches of the f-holes (three parts):

| Violin | Viola | Cello |
|--------|-------|-------|
| 19.5 cm | 21.9 cm | 41.7 cm |

Distance from the edge of the table to the nut (two parts):

| Violin | Viola | Cello |
|--------|-------|-------|
| 13 cm | 14.6 cm | 27.8 cm |

In practice, and particularly in France, the second way is used, taking as the point of division the rib, which gives a more constant base than the purfling, the position of which is not fixed. Then again in practice, especially during construction, the division is thus: first from the nut to the rib; second from the edge of the table to the inside notches of the f-holes.

After some years agreement has gradually been reached on the stop of the instruments of the quartet, especially in France and England. In spite of this, a lot of instruments with odd stops are still around.

The measurements that best answer the needs of performance and are most in harmony with the average dimensions of the hand are:

|  | Nut to rib: | Edge to f's (Notches): |
|--|-------------|------------------------|
| Violin: | 5 pouces, -2 lignes [ 131 mm ] | 7 pouces, +3 lignes [ 196 mm ] |
| Medium Viola: | 5 pouces, +3 lignes [ 142 mm ] | 8 pouces [ 216 mm ] |
| Large Viola: | 5 pouces, +4 lignes [ 144 mm ] | 8 pouces, +1 ligne [ 219 mm ] |
| Medium Cello: | 10 pouces, +4 lignes [ 280 mm ] | 14 pouces, +10 lignes [ 401 mm ] |
| Large Cello: | 10 pouces, +5 lignes (barely) [ 281 mm ] | 15 pouces [ 406 mm ] |

It will be noted that the measurements above are given in *pouces* and *lignes*; French lutherie is even today [1910] using exclusively our old system of measures. It is easy to convert these to the metric system by remembering that the number of divisions in the unit is twelve and that the *ligne* contains about 2.255 millimeters. [ As I have done above.]

# CHAPTER IV

THE FINGERBOARD PROJECTION AND ITS CONSE-QUENCES: HEIGHT OF THE STRINGS OVER THE FIN-GERBOARD; THEIR ANGLE OVER THE BRIDGE. DIMENSIONS OF THE BRIDGE.

Formerly the fashion was to keep the necks thick in the front, the fingerboards very low, the strings light, and the tone moderate.

It is in these terms that Lupot, via Abbot Sibire, portrays the way our ancestors set up their violins, and the amount of tension that exactly met the needs of performance in that period. The need to increase the string tension by a heightened fingerboard projection, and thus to increase the strength of the bar and the gauge of the strings, is due in large part to the advances in instrumental technique that were accelerated by the modern music movement. Excursions into the upper registers, rapid execution of passages, brilliant tone, facility and variety in bow strokes, all this would be impossible on instruments set up in the old way. Our ancestors were not deprived; their technique answered the needs of their music.

If this transformation was accomplished quite quickly in the instrument, that was not the case with the bow.

It is enough to glance back from about 1600 to the end of the 18th century to follow its development, or I might say, its embryology:

**Mersenne** (1620), a primitive form, with all the weight at the butt end, headless, the extreme end makes a hook in front.
**Kircher** (1640), the same shape, but there is a hint of a head.
**Castrovillari** (1660), there is the beginning of a head, and along with this more elasticity in the stick.

**Bassani** (1680), the same shape, somewhat more accentuated.
**Corelli** (1700), The head is born, shaped like a *swan's neck*, the frog is finished, the bow is short but balanced; the short ribbon of hair is parallel to the stick.

**Tartini** (1740), the same shape, more pronounced; the stick is of a good length.

**Cramer** (1770), a radical change has been made, the head has lost the swan's neck shape and become *square*: this is the modern bow.

**Viotti** (1790), the bow reaches its full perfection with **Tourte, Sr.**, then **Tourte, Jr.** (1747-1835). Plate I.

As we see, the bow was transformed in parallel with the evolution of music.
The desertion of the harpsichord and invention of the pianoforte, then the piano, then the powerful modern piano, and

the enlargement of the concert halls necessitated a stronger sound on the part of the bowed instruments.

If someone really wanted to give an accounting of what the old music was like, he would have to perform with an A of 808 vibrations, and the timbre of the instruments provided with such lightly stretched strings would marry admirably with that of the harpsichord. To present this music with modern intensity is to perpetrate a despicable anachronism.

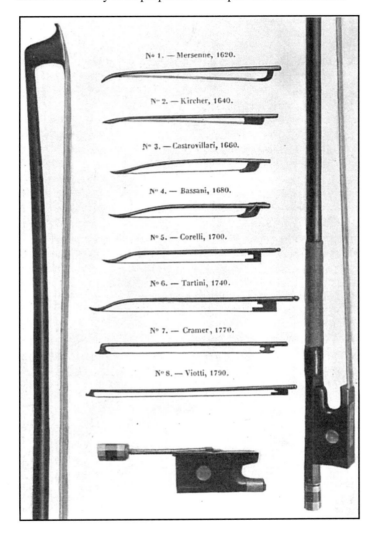

PLATE I. THE BOW: ITS EVOLUTION AND IMPROVEMENT, FROM THE BEGINNING OF THE 18TH CENTURY TO OUR TIME.

The knowledge of these details leads us to explain a singular phenomenon, of which many were victims unaware:

Have you ever been called to play in a hall or somewhere that you've never been before, without introduction, and put in the presence of a piano that was to be used for accompaniment, tuned below the normal pitch? You then lowered the tuning of your violin, and from the outset, you found yourself bothered by the poor quality of your playing and by your lack of skill: your left hand was heavy, no tone, no brilliant passages, bow strokes misfiring for no apparent reason. If you are neither a keen observer nor a vain person you attributed your poor performance to a temporary indisposi-

tion. All the trouble came from the fact that your violin had lost its good qualities, just as a razor's edge is blunted by the blows of a hammer. In the modern violin the tension of the strings through the fingerboard projection, and the resistance of the table through the dimensions of the bar, demand that the tuning be based on the A of 870 vibrations. The bow too is balanced with a view to this general tension. [This is a little lower than 880 Herz, i.e. our A-440.]

As a rule then, always check the tuning of the piano and, if it's abnormal, cancel your performance rather than subject yourself to an unfair review.

The fingerboard projection determines the angle formed by the strings over the bridge and as a result their tension, likewise the force of the bridge on the table. The higher the fingerboard projection, the higher the bridge will be; the angle formed by the strings will be sharper and consequently the force higher.

There are various ways to set the fingerboard projection. The usual and the most practical way to check it is the following:

A rule is held on the fingerboard with the left hand, then, with the right hand, a small graduated rule is placed perpendicular to the table at the *point* (middle of the imaginary line that goes from the notch of one f-hole to the other). Where it intersects with the first rule, it indicates a certain number of millimeters or lignes, which will be the proper measurement of the fingerboard projection, if the instrument is well adjusted.

The best measurements are the following:

| | | |
|---|---|---|
| Violin: | 12 ½ lignes (or just over) | [ 28 mm] |
| Viola: | 14 ½ lignes | [ 33 mm] |
| Cello: | 3 pouces, 1 ½ ligne (barely) | [ 84 mm] |

[These are just slightly higher than the typical modern figures, 27, 32, and 81 mm in *Useful Measurements for Violin Makers*.]

It is obvious that these measurements should be reduced for small instruments.

Under these conditions, the most desirable height of the strings over the [end of the] fingerboard would work out to:

Violin, from the fingerboard to the . . . . . . . . . . . . E: 4 mm
" . . . . . . . . . . . . . . . . . . . . . . . . . . . . . . . . . . . . . . . G: 5 mm
Viola, from the fingerboard to the . . . . . . . . . . . A: 4.5 mm
" . . . . . . . . . . . . . . . . . . . . . . . . . . . . . . . . . . . . . . C: 5.5 mm
Cello, from the fingerboard to the . . . . A: 5.7 mm (barely 6)
" . . . . . . . . . . . . . . . . . . . . . . . . . . . . . . . . . . . . C: 7 mm

At the same time we come to determine the height of the bridge; it remains to indicate the thicknesses that experience has shown to be the most suitable:

| Thickness: | At the feet | At the top |
|---|---|---|
| Violin | 4 mm | 2 mm |
| Viola | 5 mm | 2 mm + |
| Cello | 12 mm | 3 mm |

The bridge represents the bisector of the angle formed by the string, and consequently, the resultant of the forces pulling on these strings.

Note: The term bisector is not rigorously exact. In reality, if the bridge is perpendicular to the table, one of the angles, that on the tailpiece side, is noticeably smaller than the other. Were the end of the fingerboard raised up from the table an amount approximately equal to that of the tailpiece, the angles would be equal, or nearly so, if the strings touched the fingerboard as they touch the tailpiece, but since they are raised up a few millimeters, an appreciable difference results. Fig. 2.

The formation of this angle is the final reason to calculate the fingerboard projection, since it will more or less establish the

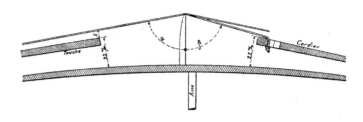

bridge height over the table and the overall tension. The ideal angle will then be the one that gives the required and sufficient force. Fig. 3.

An instrument meeting the above conditions, and having normal arching and graduation, should have the following

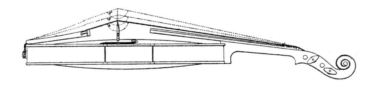

number of degrees:

| Violin | 155 degrees |
|---|---|
| Viola | 154 degrees |
| Cello | 150 degrees |

For the small instruments, this angle can be more obtuse, and thus the projection should be lower.

[These angles are somewhat sharper than in my book *Useful Measurements for Violin Makers*. They will be less so toward the treble side and with steel strings. The exact angle should not be taken too seriously; it is really the result rather than the cause of other things being correct. M. Greilsamer's treatment is cited in the bibliographies of Leipp's *Le Violon* and Sacconi's *I "Segreti" di Stradivari*, in Millants' *Manuel Practique de Lutherie*, page 122, and in Roussel's *Grundlagen der Geige und des Geigenbaues*, page 25.]

# CHAPTER V

## THE BAR AND THE POST.

In the ignorance that prevailed after the decline of Italian lutherie of the factors governing the acoustic qualities of bowed instruments the organ that was the most tortured, with the purpose of obtaining from it powers that it never had, is undeniably the *bar*.

There are two kinds of bar theorists, the deductive, who see a secret in the way the ancients barred their instruments, a lost secret like that of the varnish but more important, according to them, and the inductive, convinced *a priori* that changing the shape or position of the bar, or both at the same time, ought to result in the improvement of any instrument.

The partisans of the so-called lost secret, if they are reasonable, should yield to the following simple argument: If the ancients had possessed a secret of barring, lost today, their instruments ought to sound bad when fitted with modern bars. But it's the opposite that happens.

The second kind has included both renowned and stubborn researchers. Savart, an admirable theorist, but mediocre in practice, was, I believe, the first researcher in this direction:

"One could," he said, "replace the bar with a support made in a circular arc which touched the table at only one point, the ends of which were attached to the inside of the blocks. I have tried this several times, and did not notice that the tone was changed. This would be a means of having instruments of great solidity and whose tone would last a long time without changing, but it must be noted that it is very hard to determine the dimensions of a support like this because they could not be the same for all violins, since stiffness is so variable in wood; this problem exists with the ordinary bar too, but it is less critical."

The luthier Rambeaux had the idea of attaching a lengthwise bar to the back of the instrument, symmetrically opposite to the one glued to the sound board.

Here is what M. Fetis said when called upon at that time to pronounce on the merits of the invention:
"One of the exhibitors, M. Rambeaux of Paris, has conceived the notion of gluing a second bar to the back of the violin, on which the post is placed. According to the testimony of some distinguished artists who have tried the instrument (originally less satisfactory), its tone production was easy, even, and the fourth string in particular had a remarkable tone. It seemed to us that this effect had to be produced through the coincident energetic vibrations of the two bars, rendered normal [?] under the control of the post. We believe that an instrument built of the best material and with the perfection in detail that their products carry does not need this appendage, but recent experiments done in our presence show that there can be a noticeable improvement in lesser instruments. . ."

At the Exposition of 1867, M. Miremont exhibited a violin fitted with a second bar.

M. Gallay accounts for the innovation in the terms:

"We reserve our appraisal of the interior modification for which, we have been told, M. Miremont has received a patent. We were told of a second bar. If it's a matter of a second bar going from the upper block to the lower, it would be reminiscent of a system already conceived and proposed to the Gand brothers about fifteen years ago by an American luthier.
"Before adopting this system and wishing to learn the effects of this peculiar fixture, the Gands agreed to set up some violins in this fashion, but the results were in no way conclusive.
"The inventor especially wished to avoid the movement of the fingerboard projection that occurs sometimes on certain instruments, when, as a result of the pull of the tailpiece, the neck is pulled forward thus lowering the fingerboard; moreover, this supplementary bar would have the advantage of better sound distribution and prevention of bad notes."

M. Mordret, who was unaware of the work of M. Gallay had, in 1865, done similar experiments on his own, which he expressed thus:

"The fixture consists in a rod of spruce traversing the inside of the box and mortised into the ends of the two blocks; we have calculated the shape and dimensions for resistance to bending, the same over its whole length.

"From the viewpoint of solidity, the result was what it should be, but from the viewpoint of sound, we were wrong in our expectation. The timbre and power did not change noticeably; but some notes, particularly among those on the fourth string, exhibited pulsating vibrations, whose effect was quite disagreeable. [ We call these "wolf tones." ] This phenomenon is explained thus: it results from too great a mobility in the sound board, having become isolated as a result of the rigid connection of the neck with the tailpiece. It produces these gratuitous jumps or nuisance effects, which was thoroughly understood by M. Savart when he said that the vibration of the box ought never take control of that of the strings.

"And so, little encouraged by the result, we abandoned our experiments."

These failures, which belong to the past, are not meant to discourage research on the bar. But every day we hear of a new patent, of a sensational new discovery, and I hardly think that any of them has yet changed a "Vinaigrius" of (insert the name of your choice), into an authentic Stradivarius. To adequately account for the fanciful character of such researches that are preordained to fruitlessness, it is enough to review the very origin of the violin. Only someone who, like Savart, facing the inability to reproduce what the ancients did, studied other forms governed by other principles, would be able to justify trying to change the bar at the same time. If he succeeded in producing an instrument having new qualities, he would enrich the string quartet with a new instrument that was no longer a violin.

Our bar is exactly similar to that of Maggini, Amati, Stradivari, with this difference that, calculated for a greater fingerboard projection, it is stronger and longer. If the ancients had our A, they would have done as we have. All the old Italians have gained from rebarring, and it is certainly thanks to this that we can appreciate the quality of these instruments now adapted to the requirements of modern music.

It would seem redundant to conclude that this same modern bar, which is fine in a fine Cremona, could not be bad in another instrument, but it does not follow that therefore it should also be put into our own fine Cremona.

This begging of the question is the mistake made by all those who have wanted to impose on the bar a role that doesn't belong to it.

Why then seek to improve an organ that provides perfect results in perfect instruments? Good instruments give their maximum output when they are well barred, and their least when the contrary is true, but from the beginning they are good for different reasons, which all have their proportionate influence: it is in the architecture and the varnish that we also have to look.

The position of the post and its length play a great part in the final adjustment. The center of the post should be on a line parallel to the axis of the instrument, passing through the middle of the right foot of the bridge (on the side opposite the bar), 4 to 5 mm behind it for the violin, 5 to 5.5 mm for the viola, and 7 to 8 mm for the cello. Its length must be such that, placed perpendicular to the two tables, it will stay in this position without force.

Such are the theoretical conditions that apply for a properly placed post. In practice, nothing is more difficult than to find the exact point, the only one that answers the temperament of the instrument.

And it is said that nearly always the one who performs this delicate operation does not play the violin, and is consequently unable to appreciate the quality of his work.

On the other hand, there are players that spend their life changing the position of this post without thereby modifying by an atom the nature of their instrument or their talent.

When searching for the position of the post, this is the principle to follow:

*If the post is moved toward the bridge, the higher strings gain in brilliance to the detriment of the lower, and if it is moved away, the opposite happens.*

———————

# CHAPTER VI

## ABOUT AN INTERNATIONAL VIOLIN MAKING COMPETITION. WHO IS THE BEST JUDGE?

The Italian newspapers told us recently of substantial wagers made on particularly original conditions. It was a question of telling, in a single hearing, a hundred sou violin from an authentic Stradivarius. It seems that it was the five franc violin that got all the votes, in that it was well and truly taken for the Stradivarius. I will be willing to bet myself, nevertheless, that the unfortunate owner of the Cremona did not ask to trade his instrument for the other. It is worth noting that the same newspapers were silent about the name and address of the house that delivers such masterpieces so cheaply. I am familiar with this country in which the commercial advertisement had been the first and last reason for this singular, or if you prefer, this peculiar contest.

We were invited on the 5th, 6th, and 7th of January, 1909, in the Salle Gaveau, to a struggle of this kind, but on a different and higher level, which everyone took seriously. Luthiers internationally were invited to compete, and many answered the call.

Ten old violins and eight semi-modern violins equally took part in the trial of which the final result was:

| | |
|---|---|
| No. 1 | A modern violin |
| No. 2 | A Stradivarius |
| No. 3 | A modern violin |
| No. 4 | A Guadagnini |
| No. 5 | A Guarnerius (Joseph del Gesu) |
| No. 6 | A Montagnana |
| " | A Guarnerius (Joseph del Gesu) |
| " | A Modern violin. |

I regret that I cannot give the names of those competing, the list not having been made public, which is certainly an injustice; the unhappy losers of the final match would have at least found there, also, their small share of legitimate publicity.

Having embarked on a deeper examination of this sort of "plebiscite", I would like to point out an indirect result for which there is room to rejoice, that is to attract new public attention to the charm of beautiful voice and timbre, and to take the musicians themselves back to wholesome traditions, to the love of what we call tone quality. For the growing indifference to the intrinsic beauty of sound, practiced by the producer as well as by the consumer, has several causes. Modern music, with its radical innovations and the profound shifts in its writing, holds our spirit in constant unrest, and absorbs it to the point that the ear becomes no more than a neutral intermediary, taking almost no part in the feast for which it was destined. It seems thus to escape the domain of sense and become, for some, a pure joy of the spirit, a kaleidoscope of intellectual and ingenious combinations, for others, a sentimental abstraction that allows spiritual meanings rather than material realizations. On the other hand, certain composers, wishing to clothe their thought in an absolutely new form, try to reduce the role, too important to please them, of the quartet in the orchestra and find in transferring the lead to other families of instruments original effects and color. Such attempts are legitimate and useful; they are sure to give birth to a harvest of which we are given to taste only the first sometimes sour fruits, but the bowed instrument, bequeathed us by the old master luthiers of Italy, after centuries of fumbling lives on nevertheless as the most perfect of all instruments, and to let it fall into disrepute would amount to an immediate return to barbarism.

The experiment which we came to attend has precedents that are renowned and more typical, not involving in most instances, as today, simple copies facing their venerable originals, but instruments of new shape and construction claiming to surpass everything that had gone before.

In 1817, Chanot presented his violin to the Royal Academy of Fine Arts in Paris, before a commission composed of Gossec, Cherubini, Lesueur, Ch. de Prony, et Berton. The report concluded in these terms:
"M. Boucher, at the request of the committee, had brought to the session one of the best known Stradivaris, and as there was a very strong prejudice in favor of such excellent violins, M. Boucher, to allow it to be judged impartially, agreed to go into an adjoining room and play alternately the same passages on both instruments. *The entire commission, in three consecutive trials, believed they heard the Stradivarius when M. Boucher played the new violin and vice versa when he played the Stradivarius.*

"This continuing mistake decided the question in favor of the violin of M. Chanot, which, although made of new wood cut for two years and sold after six months, was able to sustain such stiff competition on equal grounds."

The 26th of July of the same year, a new test was requested in front the reassembled Academy. Boucher lent himself in the same way as before, the outcome was the same, and Chanot's violin was proclaimed superior to that of Stradivarius.

In 1818, Felix Savart obtained, with his trapezoidal violin a similar triumph before the Academy of Sciences. The committee was composed of Ch. de Prony, Cherubini, Catel, Berton, Lesueur, and Biot. The violinist Lefebvre was tasked with playing alternately an excellent Italian violin and that of Savart. The report concluded thus:

"It remained for us to make a final test, the more important one, and the more decisive: this would be to ask some skilled artist to try the new violin of M. Savart, comparing it with a regular violin of excellent quality. The committee asked M. Lefebvre, the orchestra leader of the Feydeau theater, if he would be willing to perform the test in our presence. M. Lefebvre yielded to our wishes with complete compliance; he successfully compared the violin of M. Savart with that which he habitually uses, and so expressively in his hands. In the beginning he played for us successively the one and the other. A great purity of tone was observed in the new violin along with perfect evenness; we know how rare and sought after this quality is; the new violin, heard thus up close, appeared to have a little less brightness than the other! To assure ourselves of the difference, we asked M. Lefebvre to go into an adjoining room, and play alternately the same phrases on both instruments, without telling us the order in which he put them; *then they were so perfectly equal that those better trained were continually confusing the one with the other*, or if the new violin presented any difference that was sometimes recognizable, it was *a little smoother in tone*."

In 1832, the Academy of sciences and arts in Milan judged with like enthusiasm the results of C. A. Galbusera, and the musical press of the period was unstinting in praise for the perfection of this new violin.

In 1867, an amateur of Grenoble, more modest, believed only that he had found the varnish of the old Italian makers. He presented the result of his discovery to the Statistical Society of sciences and arts of Grenoble, which published the same year a "report on the varnish invented by M. Grivel". This report, after having observed that the Grivel varnish was identical in appearance to the Cremonese, ended with a comparison of the sound and tone quality of M. Grivel's violins and the Italian instruments, a comparison that was thoroughly to the credit of the inventor.

These names, these instruments, have fallen into oblivion. Today an instrument of Chanot or Savart would not be bought except as an object of curiosity.

The quotes that I am giving are not to denigrate the judges of that time. Quite the opposite. I only think that, given, on the one hand, the unassailable choice of musicians and scholars whose integrity *a priori* confirmed their impartiality, and on the other, the bankruptcy of their judgment, there is food for thought; as to continuing these experiments, it is better to ask ourselves if they are possible, up to what point, and under what conditions. If we succeed in establishing the givens of the problem, we will know why the past events have been contradictory, and we will be able to predict the results that could be given in the future by this kind of comparison.

Having occupied ourselves with the ear as a judge, we begin to see a little of what happens with the other senses, sight, for example.

Those who are called on to judge precious materials, metals or stones, have, in addition to their senses, testing methods that taken together form a certain *criterion*. With the help of chemical reactions, the microscope, the precision balance scale, etc., they can determine in an absolute way the nature, purity, density, type of molecular structure and crystalliza- tion, refraction, hardness, etc., etc. That these various tests may be made by many people or by only one, in a longer or shorter time, does not matter to the result. One would know better than to argue over the number of carats in a gold ingot, the means of verification being available to everyone, and the result completely objective.

Everyone knows that there are only a few people whose sight would be called normal. The defects that are more or less important such as color blindness, astigmatism, lack of clarity in the vitreous humor, a restricted angle of vision, defects of

the optical nerve or the retina, not to mention near- sightedness and far-sightedness, are so widespread that if we allow that 25 percent have perfect vision, we will probably be over the true figure; but then if one questioned a hundred people, he would certainly have more than three fourths that claimed in good faith to have excellent eyesight. How many young people take the railway examination and are shocked to learn that they are color blind and can't tell red from green!

Going back to the ear: Look at a full concert hall. Among those present, leaving out the sheep of Panurge [ready to do anything, like Rabelais' rogue], how many do you think have a personal opinion and are capable, not only by culture but character, of thinking for themselves? A fourth seems to me a fair figure. We take this fourth and ask ourselves how many there are in this intelligent group, as healthy in body as they are in spirit, whose sense of hearing is adequate for cerebral understanding!

The following example will illustrate my thought:

A professor of the violin, a member of a respected orchestra, told me one day that a newcomer, placed at a desk in back of him, drew sounds so sour, so disagreeable, from his instrument that he could hardly bear the proximity. Now another time at home, we came to speak of the *quality of tone*, and this same artist who distilled sulfuric acid from his violin, set himself to pontificate on the question, as though he were the only one who understood it, and in fact did not express himself badly.

You see then that we are faced with the impossibility of finding qualified judges and appeal-proof judgments. The method of dealing in bowed instruments, especially in antiques, seems to provide a reason for this opinion. Indeed, the dealer always sells the name, never the quality. Why? because the brand, not the quality, has a commercial value, and because the dealer that undertakes to guarantee the one knows very well that he cannot guarantee the other.

You would not ask twenty thousand francs for a violin without a name, however good, and feel confident you had made a valid contract, whereas you will be able to take with confidence thirty thousand francs for a Stradivarius as bad, as deteriorated, as you can imagine. In the case of a lawsuit, the court will nullify the first sale, but surely validate the second.

Now, without wishing to push things to the extreme, let's take two artists called upon to choose each an instrument for his personal use. The one will, according to his personality, technique, skills, ideal, and state of his hearing, take perhaps an instrument that is powerful, robust, albeit rude and lacking in delicacy, whereas the other will prefer a gentler voice, a smoother timbre.

We always observe then that the judgment of an instrument is not purely objective. It is partly subjective, and as there is an infinite variety of nuances in the infinite variety of personalities of men and instruments, we are faced with the substantial impossibility of establishing a valid classification system. - What's the solution then? - Let's stop rationalizing and find it.

Leaving behind our direct or indirect interests, which have a very fair amount of influence on our way of seeing and hearing, our attachments, friendships, likes, dislikes; accounting only for the numerous differences in the characteristics of the ear, general physical characteristics, individual technique, temperament, and taste: does it not seem then that anyone driven by the desire to own an instrument, in buying and paying for it, makes a particularly significant judgment?

I don't want to claim that fashion plays a role, and that those who sell many, have more talent than those who sell fewer. That would go against the grain. What does it matter to me if house X sells a lot of chocolate, if at the time I prefer that of house Y? The posters, the advertisements, the premiums, the commissions paid to brokers for offering me item X, will they change my taste? Chocolate. . . . Violins. . . Isn't it the same thing?

And now the conclusion appears to flow naturally:

*The only person qualified to judge an instrument is the one who bought that instrument with his own funds for his personal use. All judgments, made outside of these two conditions, are tainted with legitimate suspicion.*

But, you are about to exclaim, a parallel conclusion implies the impossibility of recognizing a bad instrument from a good one, and makes its qualities reside not in the object, but in the imagination of the player or listener! Nevertheless, the Cremonas enjoyed such a reputation after about three centuries... -- Very true. We have come to study only one side of the question: the comparison. And you see, your objection once again supports our conclusion. While Stradivarius himself was alive, artists were very divided about his work. Many preferred the different Amatis, others the German Stainer, others again the old Maggini, and in our day there is always the same division. Certain virtuosos avidly seek the instruments of Joseph Guarnerius to the exclusion of all others, etc.

If the comparison and choice are, as we have come to convince ourselves, uniquely subjective, it is not the same with the *quality*. There is a set of factors that make an instrument incontestably good. Can all these factors be defined and tested? How, with what, under what conditions? The study of one such problem is the necessary complement to the question that occupies us, and we will embark on it in the next chapter.

———————

## CHAPTER VII

### CERTAIN SIGNS OF EXCELLENCE IN AN INSTRUMENT

We have seen that the quality of an instrument is determined at the time of construction and by the adjustment. A violin may be excellent in workmanship and varnish, but if it is badly barred, if the stop is non-standard, the fingerboard projection abnormal, if the fingerboard is poorly fitted, if the bridge lacks the right proportions, if the post is not in the right place, and finally, if it is fitted with bad strings, it will be unfit for any artistic performance.

Assuming then for the moment a perfectly adjusted instrument, we ask ourselves what *criterion* serves as a basis for the connoisseur to make a judgment on the good qualities or the defects with which the instrument is endowed,

You might say at once that the maxim: "There is nothing perfect in this world" applies also to what we usually call the "king of instruments." In the most perfect violin, as with the best endowed person, the very excess of certain qualities becomes a fault. Therefore, we should not push too far the study of such subtleties, or we might be unable to formulate any positive rule. We grant as theoretically ideal an instrument that would combine all those qualities, without one dominating the others, a coincidence that will probably never be realized. The predominance of certain qualities over others, or rather to the detriment of some others, is what determines the personality of the instrument, and causes it to be chosen by the artist as best answering to his nature, temperament and aspirations. For example, de Beriot played a Maggini all his life, Paganini a Guarneri; Vieuxtemps' instrument of choice was a Guarneri, that of de Sarasate was a Stradivari; Servais used a cello of Stradivari through his whole career, of the very large pattern. . . . I know artists who often change their instruments.

If it is difficult to find in the same instrument all those qualities that merit its being called good, it is not, on the other hand, very easy to define most of those qualities the perception of which is in the domain of the senses and which the ear alone can perceive and analyze. The most precise terms will only be understand by one who plays a bowed instrument, and he will appreciate them in direct proportion to his technical instruction.

What is demanded of an instrument, first and above all, is *beauty of tone*, represented by power with resulting range, roundness, sweetness, purity, evenness, and timbre.

Experienced instrumentalists will easily agree in noting the absence or presence of these factors, with one exception: the *timbre*. Failing to agree on the significance of this term and to precisely understand its meaning, the same musicians will deliver diametrically opposite judgments. They will appraise differently the musical value of an instrument, because they let their taste speak and their personal preference prevail, and where they will find a superiority, she or he will allow no difference.

# Catalog of Professional
# Books for Violin Makers
### and for Anyone Working with or Interested
### in Bowed Instruments

Henry Strobel, Violin Maker & Publisher
10878 Mill Creek Road
Aumsville OR 97325 USA

Books@HenryStrobel.com

www.HenryStrobel.com

**METHOD :**

**or money order**

ment for the TOTAL
postage by CHECK or
on a US bank to:

Publisher
ville OR

- - - - - - - - - - - - - - - -

( )Visa ( )Amex

_____ - _____

_ Date_____

to:

Publisher
ville OR

(708) 575-5367

- - - - - - - - - - - - - - - -

LINE at:

bel.com

# THE STROBEL VIOLIN BOOK SERIES —
## — PROFESSIONAL, CONCISE, CONVENIENT

**VIOLIN MAKING, STEP BY STEP** Second edition of this

fundamental book. A complete, traditional method. Brief descriptions of alternate methods. From sharpening tools to adjustment and varnishing. Full-size drawings for making a Stradivari-style violin. Illustrated with 115 photographs of the *model violin*, and of the *demonstration violin* as it was made ("step by step") by Henry Strobel. For the violin maker or the interested violinist . . . . . . $29.50

**VIOLA MAKING, STEP BY STEP** First edition

In the same format as *Violin Making, Step by Step* (required) and *Cello Making, Step by Step*. It includes full size drawings for an elegant smaller viola, as well as information on a wide range of viola styles, sizes, and related considerations. For use with *Violin Making, Step by Step*, and keyed to it, without duplication . . . . . . . . . . . . . $25.00

**CELLO MAKING, STEP BY STEP** Third edition (Includes 4/4, 7/8 Cello Drawings). Similar to *Violin Making, Step by Step* (required), and keyed to it, without duplication. Full-size drawings for cello and inside mold. The process of making and adjusting a master cello, including alternate tools and techniques, is described in detail, with numerous photographs . . . . . . . . . . $29.50

**ART & METHOD OF THE VIOLIN MAKER** Second (Revised and Expanded) edition. Design: the violin's outline, scroll, geometry, æsthetics. Wood: species, selection, figure, cut and orientation. Making: mold types, antique & modern methods. Ribs, corners, graduation, barring, selected repairs, etc. Creativity and copying, fads and fundamentals. Illustrated with over seventy photos and diagrams. For the violin maker, repairer, and connoisseur . . . . . . . . $19.50

**USEFUL MEASUREMENTS FOR VIOLIN MAKERS** Fourth

edition of this classic handbook. A standard reference, unique and comprehensive. For violin, viola, cello, bass and bows, all sizes. Size and adjustment. Tables and text. Concise explanations. Bridge templates. Violin and cello adjustment diagrams. Illustrated $12.50

**VIOLIN MAKER'S NO**

of this sh bows. Re cracks. photogra Orientati bibliography for the co

**HEALTH OF THE VIO**

"Practica Maintena Bowed I: Translate original I

**REFLECTIONS, PERSO** Henry Strobel. Literar First Edition of 500 nu

MY F Henry for ov and t rental etc. provic musicians, teachers, an

**"WATCH ME MAKE A**

Makin: Strobel procedur Detailed supplements the "step DVD Video *or* NTSC

## WE ALSO PUBLISH TH

**HOW TO IMPROVE T: MUSICAL INSTRUMEN WOLF NOTES** By Prof.

**PRACTICAL ACOUST VIOLIN FAMILY** By Ja:

**SETUP AND REPAIR OPTIMUM SOUND** Fir David Brownell and V 375 pages, 8.5 x 11 in. sound optimization. O:

**"Coda" to Setup and**

**The Art of Violin }** Edition, In color . . . .

To put it precisely: we can distinguish two elements in the timbre, *richness* and *nature*. The richness depends on the greater or lesser quantity of certain harmonics vibrating to the exclusion of others at the same time as the fundamental tone, whereas the nature is due to the predominance of some of these harmonics over others. Appreciating the richness is a question of education of the ear, judging the nature is a matter of personal taste. Thus all objective judgment ought to be restricted to appreciation of the richness. As for the nature, we can say: I don't care for this timbre; or again: I prefer this timbre, and that's that. *To each his own...*
[The distinction suggested here between partials and their amplitudes does not seem very helpful.]

To an experienced ear, the nature of the timbre varies not only from maker to maker (for example a Nicolo Amati differs in this respect completely from a Joseph Guarneri), but again with the same maker, who has never made two identical instruments. It is chiefly, disregarding other details, the nature of the timbre that guides the players in their selection, and makes each have a preference for this or that maker. It is a phenomenon of likes and dislikes like that of odors.

By the word *power* we mean that the instrument ought never stagger under the bow, but answer its demands with unlimited generosity, to the point of appearing to the performer as endowed with an inexhaustible reserve of sound. Power results in *range*. On this subject, inexperienced artists experience the deception of observing that their instruments, apparently formidable under the ear, do not carry in the concert hall, whereas others that seem less loud when played transmit all the way to the back of the most vast building the purity of a note produced by the slightest brush of the bow. These latter are in reality the powerful ones. They send forth a *pure* tone, free of all extraneous noise, whereas, in the others confused noises, mixed with the tone, strike the nearby ear, and make the sound seem very loud. From a few meters away, the noise is hardly noticed, the tone is deprived, and the acoustic poverty of the instrument is pitifully evident.

The sound should be neither dry, nor nasal, nor hollow, nor wooly; a good instrument should have its sound *outside* and not inside. An error, which has spread from the beginning of the nineteenth century until our time, consists in believing that highly arched instruments have *a priori* an "inside" sound. This explains the colossal number of violins flat as bedbugs that are found the world over. It is enough, however, to look with a little care at an antique of a good name to convince oneself of the opposite. The fine Italian instruments all have, without exception, pronounced archings. It is unnecessary to add that they are admirably designed.

It is difficult to define the *roundness* of a sound, but it can be understood by saying the opposite, that a round sound is the opposite of a thin sound.

By *sweet* is meant not just the opposite of sour. Sweetness, when it is a question of sound, does not imply the idea of weakness. A sweet sound should lack neither force nor range.

When, next to a full and brilliant note, there is found a weak and thin note, the instrument lacks *evenness*.

Beyond the qualities that we have now enumerated, there is one that is so to speak the crowning of the others:

It is necessary that in the higher positions, on the chanterelle as well as on the G, however small a portion of the string is vibrating, it should respond to the slightest brush of the bow with a pure and continuous tone.

In addition to these requirements that specifically concern the beauty of tone, there are those that concern performance.

Every instrument *ought to* be free of rolling ["wolf"] notes. Notes more generally subject to this fault are:

For the violin:   A, B flat, C on the fourth string.
                  B flat, C, C sharp on the chanterelle.

For the cello:   F, F sharp on the third string.

Then too it must stay in tune. The opposite indicates that the table is too thin or of too soft wood, unless the neck is not properly mortised and glued. This last defect can be repaired; as for the first, it is incurable.

If we add that all the notes should respond instantly to the most delicate invitation of the bow, that the instrument should render just as easily the slow as the brisk, ring as clearly in all keys, in C minor as in A major, for example, vibrate as easily at the attack of only one string as of several at a time, yield with ease to the different bow strokes, staccato, sautille, arpeggios, etc., we will have established the rest of what constitutes a good instrument.

————

# CHAPTER VIII

## SHORTCUTS: BAKING THE WOOD, STAINING WITH BICHROMATE.

To what extent, and under what conditions, and why, did J.B. Vuillaume heat the wood before using it, and what percentage of the instruments he put into circulation were so treated? You see, these are points on which we have no more than vague ideas. We will welcome anyone who will bring us such samples of the work of this luthier, work that appears typical, stripped today of the legends that his craft was known to create, and separated from the intense advertising that his son-in-law, the violinist Alard, and his friend Vidal, spread about him.

While awaiting the items of this process, I may be permitted to make some reflections on the question of the heating [baking or kiln drying] of wood in lutherie, and take this occasion to prove the inanity of the charges regularly brought with the jealous agreement of every colleague who rises a little over his level. The perennial poisoned arrow: *"He uses baked wood! He sterilizes his wood!"* is a calumny that is all the more difficult to defend against, since it is insinuated in the spirit of the meanly informed. The amateur and the artist capable of forming a well founded opinion are rare.

People are always inclined to believe the one who tells them: beware this instrument, it is too good for a new instrument; it will probably promptly lose all its good characteristics. Not only do they carelessly pick up this kind of thinking, which, rigorously, might be able to pass for a legitimate caution, but leap to the last limit of the absurd in choosing a poor instrument, which they hope to see improve, whether by prolonged use, or by a special providence reserved for violins poor in sound, just like that which looks after men poor in spirit. This is not all; they go even farther into the domain of the inconsistent: someone acquires an instrument fifty or a hundred years old, hard, harsh, the wood sounding as on the first day. What does anyone hope to get from such a course? Does he expect to work the miracle in his life that two generations could not achieve, after a century of patience and efforts?

The human mind does take some baffling turns: to avoid a new instrument that is good, on the pretext that it will worsen, to acquire an instrument old or new, but bad, in the hope of improving it, this is to put the *piquette* [marc brandy or grappa] in the cellar with the intention of making it an excellent *clos de Vougeot*. [a classic burgundy]

To go back to Vuillaume, it may be that at one time in his career he used baked wood to study its sound. In this case, he was able to quickly convince himself that the *baked wood had completely lost its tone quality*. This wood is dead. The tone is flat, poor, lacking refinement, timbre, and volume. Now, Vuillaume was too intelligent to stick to a path on which he would have had everything to lose. If we add that at that time you could buy old wood by the wagon load, and we know that he bought it but did not prefer it to new wood air dried for some years, we can be certain that it was not to improve the tone of his instruments that he heated his wood. I

would more willingly believe that in the beginning of his career, financially poor, but rich in artifices, he had not yet discovered the process of staining, which, in the imitations from his hand, has the twofold effect of aging the wood in the areas of wear, and of muting the rawness of the color in the varnish. To get the best price he had to quickly age the wood, and it didn't matter if heating it was the only immediate means he knew to arrive at his goal. Perhaps he did it at this time.

I will say in passing that Vuillaume somewhat later signed instruments that were not baked, but bent, that is to say, whose archings were artificially established with a press, not carved with the gouge. I will add, without trying to deepen the question, that these instruments appear to belong to the class of those that were made for the trade, and very probably without its knowledge.
[Various bending and/ or pressing processes have been used in various periods and countries in the manufacture of cheap instruments.]

To give before varnishing a golden undertone, which, without hiding the grain of the wood, permits the use of colored varnish for such reflections as are seen on the old instruments, is, you see the problem that modern making has always sought to solve, even for cheap instruments. It is even more preoccupied with this than with tone; the dealers know too well that the trained ear is rare, and that buyers are far more concerned with the appearance.

Accordingly, I must point out a method that was used for this purpose for a very long time at Mirecourt and elsewhere. I would like to believe that it has really been discontinued, and that no one does it any more: *that is the use of bichromate.*

A very concentrated solution of potassium bichromate is prepared in boiling water. Then with a large brush one or more coats are applied to the violin in the white. At first the wood takes on a bright yellow tone, then, with exposure to light and drying, it turns brown, and finally it mimics the appearance of age. Bichromate has also the advantage of bringing out the flame of the maple: almost to the point where it appears as if the material used was of an exceptionally high quality.

Up till now that's fine. Except that there is a *but*: luthiers or violin manufacturers have a habit of sealing the table with gelatine to keep the varnish from soaking in. Now the bichromate, with which the table is saturated, acts on the gelatine with the same chemical reaction used by taxidermists: everyone knows that animal parts soaked in a bichromate solution are petrified in a few days, and are preserved indefinitely from the air.

What happens to the violin? The more it is played, the more it is exposed to light, the more the bichromate makes its action felt on the gelatine with which the table is coated, and in general on the materials susceptible to attack by the bichromate which the wood naturally contains. The instrument becomes petrified, and to the extent that this phenomenon occurs, the tone the tone gets more or less sour, dry, and hissing. As mediocre as it was, the instrument has become irremediably bad, and unfit for any use.

I am sure that, among my readers, there are many who have observed the progressive demise of similar instruments without being aware of the cause.

In summary, I can say that if I believe the use of bichromate has been abandoned for expensive instruments, I am sure that heating the wood, or rather baking it, with the sole of giving it the appearance of age, is trickery used only on mass produced goods.

[Anyway there are other reasons that potassium bichromate and/or glue are less desirable primary finishing materials.]

———————

# CHAPTER IX

## NECESSARY PRECAUTIONS IN PURCHASING AN ANTIQUE

What artist or amateur has not happened, at least once in his life, to stubbornly spend a more or less large sum in the restoration of an antique, hoping, despite failures, to restore health to a decrepit violin, a veritable invalid of art, once crippled, become resistant to every remedy, and for which the very remedy becomes worse than the disease? When asked from day to day about an old violin, I frequently find myself, if it's a question of a recent purchase, in a difficult situation. Once, the object had been sold by a dealer, who, as it can happen, knew enough to write a receipt protecting him under the law from unfair hardships to an inexperienced seller. Another time, the unfortunate has an object sold to him by a layman with the best faith in the world. Often it's a buyer who believes he has acquired an instrument of great value at the expense of the seller, but has himself been cheated. Another time again, the instrument is perfectly sound, but it no longer pleases its new owner who discovers all its imaginary faults, and finally I find myself in front of a man deceived, who blames the whole world... himself excepted.

The buyer is always deceived through his own fault. Lacking specialized knowledge, ignorant of the extent of his rights, he buys under the influence of a passing and superficial fancy, and on the whole these transactions come to this: for every one luck has dealt a good hand, and who has come across a good instrument that will appreciate, there are a hundred who have made a bad investment, which sooner or later they will try to get rid of. How many will then exchange their one-eyed horse for a blind one, and pay a good price again for this new transaction? There are those who spend their life in these ruinous and deceptive pursuits. I will not speak of the few, whose ears lack conviction, and who end up by finding their instrument, bad as it may be, superior to those of others.

I will go on to try to point out the precautions one should take in buying an antique, and without claiming to give the expertise which experience and years bestow, I hope to lay down the exact elements of this issue on which most people have only the vaguest notions. We will distinguish the ethical and practical considerations one at a time, establishing a positive and definite basis for all transactions in the material of lutherie, the only safe approach for the two contracting parties.

The precarious health of antique violins is not a modern problem. These fragile structures were built to last practically forever, and they succumb rather more to poor treatment than to the ravages of time. Those instruments that are well preserved and still good are irrefutable proof of this; but on the whole, the physical decline of Cremonas had already begun within a hundred years, and led the abbot Sibire not without bitterness to say: "Violin making is perhaps the only trade in the world in which the old is consistently considered more valuable than the new and the maintenance more difficult than the building."

Since then, how many of the sick became worse from

accidents of all kinds, sometimes badly aggravated by awkward repairs! How many others, preserved by Providence from accidental trauma, are in turn emaciated by strokes of the plane at the owner's request? Then, to recover their normal thicknesses, how many of these pass into other hands graced by a kind of prosthesis called *doubling* in lutherie? Should we also mention those forgotten violins, reposing in the shelter of a comfortable attic, that have felt their ribs ruthlessly gnawed by woodworm, the enemy of every idle instrument?

To sum up, there remain few instruments that have not suffered greatly, and the number of those that have not suffered at all is necessarily very limited; even some of these are not strong enough to withstand the nervous energy of certain eager hands in their desire to draw out an improbably large sound and gradually wear out in their genteel old age.

In Abbot Sibire's time, the sharp buyer affected a certain coyness in seeking out an instrument which still had its original bar; it was for him a prime assurance on which to base his hopes. There would be no question of encountering such instrument now, and anyone who wants to be buy an antique has to arm himself with more modesty and certainly more caution than in those remote times.

The buyer nearly always is unaware that when a professional dealer sells an instrument it's a matter of authenticity and never of quality. If you ask him about this, he will answer quite rightly that tone quality is a matter of taste, and that he was not aware that this could be the object of a commercial transaction as such. He knows very well that in suits to nullify a sale, the courts will always validate the sale if authenticity is recognized rather than whether the instrument is good or bad. In short, the dealer is selling his guarantee, that is, his prestige. That is so true that, in practice, the expertise of a dealer has a value proportional to his reputation and to the size of his business, whereas the expertise of all dealers ought to have equal value.

It is important then for the buyer who wants to know what he's getting in addition to the maker's name to be familiar with all the particular things which give an antique the most points in its favor, as well as all its injuries, however well concealed by touch-up, and how they prejudice its future.

Every blemish takes away a part of its commercial value, depending on its seriousness. Nevertheless there are defects that affect only the commercial value, and have no influence on tone quality. The distinction is too easy to make to require a definition.

Assume now that we are looking at an antique instrument. The first thing we are concerned with is knowing whether it is homogeneous, that is if all its parts are from the same maker and were put together by him to create this instrument.

From the day that antiques began to be sought after, a new industry was born, and after a century it has grown in direct proportion to demand as cause and scarcity as consequence. This industry consists in combining the leftovers of several old instruments, fitting them together to make a new,

anonymous one, which is baptized according to its resemblance to this or that brand. It is from several parishes, as Abbot Sibire might have said, but one can guarantee it is old.

Suppose now that one happens to fit together leftover parts from two Stradivaris no longer having any individual worth and impossible to restore, he will have made a new Stradivarius, which he will be able to certify as such, and consequently give great value to these stray pieces.

Many violins have lost their original heads, which have been replaced with modern ones, carved more or less successfully in the desired style, or by an old one from another maker, or finally, by one from the same maker, but belonging to another instrument. It also happens often that a part of the body is replaced. A rib, the table in part or completely, on the inside the linings, blocks, etc. Whatever it may be, perfect homogeneity is something quite unusual in an antique and is not taken for granted, above all when it coincides with the absence of other defects which we will next examine.

A rather prevalent prejudice of the time expected an antique, to be worthwhile, to be decorated with cracks, and some attributed to such scars the cause of the good tone of these veterans of art. We need not belabor the naivete of such views. Nowadays an instrument without cracks is always more desirable; but as this kind of rarity is hardly to be encountered, a judgment has to be made, and we have to choose the lesser of the evils. The worst cracks are those in the table or in the back at or near the sound post. It is easy to see why: the post, subjected to the force of the bridge, will always tend to open these wounds. The stability of the instrument will be lost, and its owner will never be at peace. To correct this, the repairer undertakes one of those heroic procedures which I have already mentioned, and, not satisfied with rejoining the two parts with a little glue, he puts in what is called a *doubling*. Through the abuse of doubling, the instrument is no longer the same except in its external appearance. The whole inside may be inlaid thus with foreign parts: a *sound post patch*, in the case in question; *belly doubling*, when the table is too thin, whether as a result of the wood being too soft, or having been thinned by a vandal repairman; *edge doubling*, after the table has been removed many times and the edges are worn out; *back doubling*, to give strength to an instrument which lacks it, etc. etc.

The opposite evil to these rarely effective repairs is to be found in instruments which have been made too thin, whether through a notion of their owners or through the repairman's ignorance. In this case, a doubling is called for to restore the thickness if not elasticity to the instrument, but often the shrewd seller prefers to leave them as is, because a person does not *see* that an instrument has been thinned and may not very well *hear* it, and thus an instrument is able to pass as a virgin of repair, representing a large increase in commercial value. [Elasticity is an awkward term in violin texts; it often means stiffness with low damping.]

Repairers have a mania for unnecessarily restoring the archings of every instrument that falls under their hand. In this case, it is subject to a really extraordinary situation. Under the great pressure which is applied to the table, the wood fibers are smashed, the varnish is crushed, and as a final outcome an incoherent swelling substitutes for the previous archings, carefully calculated and executed with insight, and which from now on are forever false. A mixture is made to renew the varnish, giving it an appearance that doesn't deceive the connoisseur, and never more from its martyred breast will rise the melodious and pure voice its creator breathed into it. [It is fair to observe that the level of restoration work has risen very significantly since 1910.]

In the foregoing I have spoken of instruments that did not stay in tune, as a result of the weakness of the table. To offer a customer an instrument stricken with this illness, it is subjected to a so-called arching restoration, just as one might poke a wheezy horse with a finger for a few days before showing it. The effect of this horse doctoring is short lived, and how it cheats the buyers!

The f-holes are often, by means of a delicate repair, moved higher or lower, according to the situation, to place them at the true stop, as I explained in the chapter on the stop.

It also happens that the ribs, too often planed down as a result of many unfortunate openings, have to be restored to regain their normal height. All that is hardly conducive to good sound. As for the varnish, that precious coating, both beautiful and necessary, there are instruments on which only some traces are evident, all the rest gone after a series of touch-ups following a series of repairs.

The question of labels, though less important, is nevertheless of a certain interest. In ancient times some sought to increase the value of art objects by signing them with names more famous or more in vogue than those of the actual artists. This is what prompted Cicero to say indignantly:

*"I hate the false signatures on foreign statues."*

Without going back so far, and to stay with musical instruments, a recent book quotes on this subject a document very curious and dating from the past.

In 1685, one year after the death of Nicolo Amati, an Italian violinist named Tomasso Vitali, who was the teacher of the French violinist Senaillé, filed a suit with the Duke of Modena. The aim of the claim was to recover damages from a compatriot, who had sold him a violin as a Nicolo Amati, and carrying his label, but of which Francesco Ruggieri, called "Il Pero", was the maker.

Those who buy for their own use and wish to know precisely the nature of their acquisition should demand from the seller a certificate of the condition of the instrument as follows:

1. A guarantee of authenticity;

2. Is the instrument homogeneous in all its part or not.? In the latter case, which are the foreign parts?

3. A list of all cracks;

4. Has the instrument any doublings or not? If yes, which ones?

5. The condition of the varnish;

6. Does it stay in tune?

7. Does the label agree with the maker and correspond to the date it was made? (This is important for Stradivaris, for example, whose value and quality vary with the periods.)

The buyer, once clear on these points, will be able to concern himself solely with the quality of sound. On this subject, he will need no more guarantee than he can give himself. If he relies on himself alone while following the rules laid down in the preceding chapters, if he follows his own taste, if he avoids all middlemen, he can be sure he is not deceived.

---

# CHAPTER X

## CRACKS AND REPAIRS

To form an idea of the capability of an instrument, we have to know the state of its health. But how does one measure strength and vitality?

It seems indeed hard to discover, without removing the table, the traces of injuries and bumps it has suffered, to grasp the importance of the damage that resulted, to know how the ill was repaired, and in a word, to estimate what remains of the antique, and what condition it's in.

Now you see we are in the situation of a doctor with his patient, and like him, we will prepare our limited means of investigation.

In the foregoing chapters, we have already seen that the methodical examination of sound qualities reveals the nature of the graduation, without which it would be necessary to use calipers.

The wise Abbot Sibire, whose work is still not obsolete today except in style, wrote earlier on this question a page which is worth recalling:

"Counterfeiting of graduation is therefore easier to detect than that of currency, and to recognize the fraud, there is no more need to open the violin than to melt down the coin. The bow is the touchstone, the sound the prosecutor, the ear the judge. Now any of the following charges suffices to justify the arrest and conviction: If the table bends under the bridge, if the violin doesn't stay in tune; if its tone is muffled or gloomy, if it is tubby, unappealing and unresonant; if its graceless notes die immediately away or resist the prodding of the bow; if they prefer to be pushed along rather than march with the others; above all if the bottom string (bourdon), out of proportion with its three colleagues, delivers a big empty sound, even though made of gut and overspun; in a word, if this fourth string straining noticeably on the fifth or sounding the drum, presents to the ear a veritable explosion, or a laughable discharge, which gives this one box the air of many; then the case is closed, the fault is obvious; the plane has gone too far, the wood is gone, the back or table are too light, one or the other; the center of percussion is too thin, the radii are too thin, the whole is too thin, the sound which has no point of departure weakens and does not carry; the voice dies out for want of substance in the body of the instrument, and the weakness of the materials conclusively proves their complete worthlessness."

Thus, listening has already given us some singularly correct indications. After having listened, we now come to look, and try to see.

Do we wish to examine the interior? We provide ourselves with one of those small round mirrors, mounted on a thin stick, which are used in surgery [we would say dentistry], and put it in carefully through one of the f-holes, preferably that on the right side, without damaging the edges or scratching the varnish. Orienting the mirror and instrument in front of a window, we will see clearly reflected in the mirror a part of the table, the position of the post and its environs, the bar and the edges to some extent. It isn't needed to see the back, or at least the central part of it. Just look through one or the other of the f-holes.

The use of the mirror is ingenious, and quickly provides a first glance at the interior; it isn't enough for everything. It is often interesting to pursue the examination of the back. For that, one must "undress" the instrument. Take off the bridge, strings and tailpiece, pull out the end button, and look through its hole, having placed the f-holes toward the daylight. One then sees inside the instrument as if he were in it.

But *one sees only as much as he understands.*

It is now time to review all the more common damages and repairs, in order to recognize them when the occasion presents itself.

**The head.** - We have learned in the third chapter, that as a result of lengthening the neck, all the old violins had to be *grafted*. The process consists in placing the old head on the new neck, taking care for its back and cheeks. There remain very few antique violins that have not undergone this operation, which does not pose, when it is successful, anything inappropriate, other than from the viewpoint of beauty and strength. I am familiar however with some Stradivaris with modern stops, still having the original necks. The lengthening was achieved by an intelligent repairer, who knew to add a sole plate of a suitable thickness at the button and at the mortise of the neck. It may happen that the head has been unluckily shattered, making this whole repair impossible. Now the head has to be strong to withstand the tension of the strings and to allow the pegs to work normally; this is one of the essential requirements for the instrument to stay in tune. In this case the repairer makes a new pegbox, to the top of which he adds the original scroll. This repair can be recognized by the line where the two parts are glued together and by the difference in varnish and workmanship.

Since an original head brings a high price, it often happens that a repairer with purely commercial objectives restores ancient debris. The interior of the pegbox must be examined with care to avoid being deceived by this.

**The dimensions** - Let's go on to the sound box, the *body* as it is called. We check whether its measurements are suitable: 35.5 cm for the violin, 36 at most for a long pattern, a minimum of 35, which is already small. From 40 to 41 for the viola, and for the cello 75.5 to 76 cm represent the right size.

**The table and the back**. - The first thing we want to know is whether the table and back were made for the same instrument. To determine this we look alternately at the purfling of the one and the other. If they appear quite similar, placed the same distance from the edge, with identical points, we may have an instrument that is homogeneous in this respect, especially if there is no difference in the varnish. Otherwise, we must look more closely. Some-  times, in the case of a valuable instrument, there are old tables that have replaced the original piece. In violas and cellos, one may find

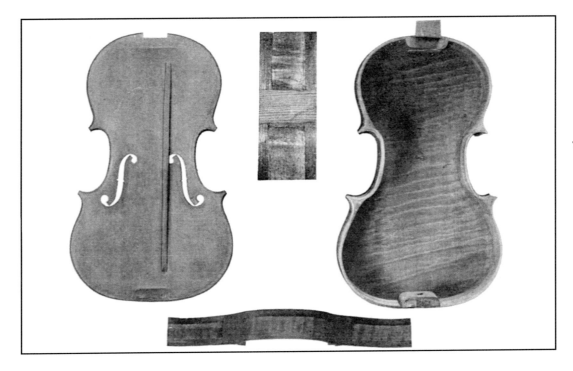

tables recut from the old *viols*. The shape, or rather its ab sence, in the very flat arching and the cut of the f-holes, betray this substitution, more common for the tables than for the backs, the former being fragile and subjected to numerous accidents. It is to Vuillaume, who shrewdly acquired all the residue from Italy and cleverly rearranged it that we owe the great number of violins, violas, and cellos, made of antique parts, it is true, but nevertheless heterogeneous. Thus in the business of lutherie he bears the inglorious but appropriate name of Harlequin.

**Cutting down and enlarging.** - Has the instrument been enlarged or reduced (cut down)? Enlargement is encountered more often in violins, the old masters having made many of these on a small pattern; cutting down and enlargement are both found often in cellos and violas, the pattern of which was unsettled for such a long time. The operation is worth the trouble: a good church bass, for example, signed with an illustrious name, but not having any commercial value because it is too large, skillfully cut down and given a normal stop, can be sold very dearly to an unsuspecting amateur.

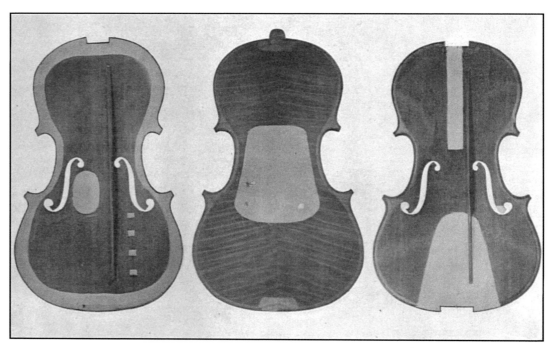

It is clear that in any case of cutting down or enlargement, one will not have an excellent instrument, the archings no longer following any design. After the repair has been done, it is quite difficult to notice, especially if one has not paid attention to the form of the archings. Here is why: a good repairer, in the one case or the other, will have taken care to preserve the original edge and purfling. One proceeds, to best carry out this task, as follows:

By means of a fine coping saw the edges, including the purfling, are separated, then, whether the size has been reduced by removing the part considered superfluous, or has been increased by gluing on a strip of wood of the desired size, the edges and purfling are readjusted. The whole is then reinforced by doubling the edges. We will see later what this involves.

Nearly always, after enlarging an antique instrument, a second purfling of the Maggini type is added to disguise the line of demarcation. Some years ago there was sold at a Druout auction a Stradivari decorated with such a superfluity.

When a repair of this kind is suspected, one can make sure by examining with an ordinary magnifying glass whether the grain of the wood continues to the edges. The grain will no longer coincide if the if the instrument has been reduced, and will agree even less if it has been enlarged. Enlargement and reduction are sometimes partial. When it is a question of widening only and not lengthening, one works at the middle. He divides the table and back into two and fills in the space. Differences in the wood and varnish betray this repair. Before proceeding to examine the inside, there still remain some details we should not overlook.

**The general condition of the varnish**. - Retouching and makeup indicate repairs or plugging of worm holes. The latter are easy to recognize. Under the varnish, we have no longer the appearance of wood, and the grain in the surrounding area is interrupted everywhere by the filler. We note in passing those instruments where the original varnish has disappeared for one reason or another, and which have been revarnished in part or totally.

**The ribs**. - It may happen that after too many openings, the ribs may become too low. Then it is necessary to raise them, that is to add a strip of maple to restore their normal height. At other times they are patched in many places.

**The button**. - The back button is frequently broken and replaced, or glued back.

**The general condition of the archings**. - If one notices abnormal swellings in the arching, a possible conclusion is that the arching has been restored. We will see what this important repair entails after we have examined the interior.

**Cracks**. - Neither varnish nor touch up can [completely] conceal cracks. When we examine the interior we will see what kind of repair they required, and to what extent they are detrimental.

**The inside of the "box"**. - With the help of a mirror, or better, looking through the hole in the lower block, as needed, we continue our investigation of the sound post area of the table and back. We have already said that cracks in this region are very bad, because they are in a highly stressed place. It then becomes necessary, when there is such a crack, or when, as a result of fumbled and frequent movements of the post, the area is worn and weakened, to install what is called a doubling.

**Doublings**. - In lutherie, a doubling is a piece of wood that is glued into the given area, after having gouged or planed it out, as the case may be. The doubling replaces, equivalently, the wood removed. For a doubling to be successful, there must be a perfect fit. As an example, let's see how a doubling is done in the area of the sound post in the table, which is called a *sound post patch*.

One makes in the specified area a gradual excavation, of an oval shape, ranging in size from that of a pigeon's egg to a hen's. The new part which is to replace the removed wood is fitted with care, glued, pressure is applied, then after a time to dry, it is planed level overall, and the thickness is set.

A doubling is easily recognized by its color that doesn't match and by the direction of the grain, which is never continuous with that of the reinforced part. In spite of staining, the doubling remains visible, and nothing can conceal it. There is an infinity of doublings, just as there is an infinity of kinds of accidents. Those which one encounters more frequently, in addition to the *sound post patch*, which is the most common of all, are:

*The joint covers, the reinforcements to the front and back of the table, the reinforcements of cheeks* that have become too thin, or which are too weak by nature, *breast patches,* whether because of a gross accident, or because the back lacks thickness in the center (a deficiency more common in backs than tables), and finally the *doubling of the edges.*

Of all these repairs, this is one that is rather difficult to recognize when the doubling, done with old wood, includes the entire surface of table or back.

Noting once again the small cleats of wood, spaced regularly to hold cracks, we will have enumerated all the elements of this repair. To account for the damage very often resulting from such jobs, which are demanding of skill and patience, it is useful to understand in a general way how they are done.

**Procedures of doubling**. - There are three ways to make a doubling: *fitting it flat on the surface, carving it to fit, and forcing the wood to fit.*

Surface fitting is done to reinforce flat parts, edges, the back button, etc. It consists in replacing with new wood the thickness that was lost through wear, weakness, etc. As it necessarily respects the original shape it is not inappropriate, except that the large amount of glue placed between the layers makes the instrument sensitive to humidity. The same objection can be made to every doubling to some extent.

Fitting by carving, which is done especially for the sound post patch, consists, after having excavated the wood, in fitting the doubling, which has been given a convexity corresponding exactly to the concavity of the excavation. It is a delicate operation, in which one proceeds feeling his way. Although to give this work all its solidity, it may be necessary to place it under pressure, it rarely results in damage to the varnish, or in a deformation of the arching.

It is the doubling with wood forced into place, especially over arched, often extended, surfaces, breast and sides, all to save appearances, which destroys irreparably the definitive style of the majority of ancient instruments.

A summary outline of this repair will complete our instruction. The part to be doubled is placed in a counter-form, which has taken its approximate form. The doubling, having a little more than the final thickness, is glued to the arched area. Then, one places on it a bag of hot sand, of the size of the doubling, and places the whole under pressure. One tightens progressively; the doubling is bent to exactly espouse the part being doubled, and the whole takes the form of the counterpart, which, as we have said, approximates that of the arching. One lets the whole dry one or two days to avoid springing back, and finally the excess wood is planed off to set the thickness. After such a torture, it is hardly surprising that the poor instrument has lost forever, and along with the freshness and elegance of its shape, the purity of its voice.

**Restoring the arching without doubling**. - It remains for me to speak of arching restoration pure and simple, of a table, for example.

To do this, one moistens for a time the inside, then lays the table on a counterpart that has been hollowed out with care, and having as much as possible in its hollow the form of the arching of the table to be re-arched. [Precise plaster casts have, of course, replaced those of carved wood.]

The rest of the operation is like that of forcing the wood to fit. A sack of hot sand is placed on the desired area, the clamp is applied, tightened, and at the end of a rather long time, the simple restoration of arching, called *remolding*, is completed.

Remolding the arching is done when the table is too weak, of a wood too soft, or collapsed, or if as a result of long use the bar has weakened, or again if one wants to repair cracks without installing a doubling, as well as to maintain a high commercial value on an expensive instrument.

It is unusual after an operation of this kind for the arching not to be distorted, the grain of the wood crushed, and the varnish injured. Asymmetrical and swelled arching are symptoms that always make us diagnose a more or less unfortunate remolding, for there are in fact no truly fortunate ones. One may add that, nine times out of ten, restoration of arching without doubling will not last. Thus, the large number of antiques that do not stay in tune, the arching giving way progressively, until the complete destruction of the relationship which must exist between the height of the bridge and the projection of the neck. At the end of some time, the bridge seems too low, the strings too close to the fingerboard, and the whole balance is disrupted. It is then necessary to start over, or decide to fit a doubling.

# CHAPTER XI

## SOME USEFUL RECOMMENDATIONS FOR THE MAINTENANCE AND CONSERVATION OF BOWED INSTRUMENTS.

When you have finished playing, wipe the instrument with a silk cloth.

♫

To "revive" the varnish, rub it with a soft, very dry chamois skin.

♫

If the pegs work poorly, clean them with very fine sandpaper, then rub them with very dry Marseille soap and go over this with a stick of fine chalk.

♫

It may happen that the strings move over the nut in jerks with disturbing creaks.
To correct this problem, one need only carefully apply a hard lead pencil to the grooves of the nut.

♫

Should the post fall, slacken the strings at once.

♫

Don't let the bridge lean forward. To right it, slacken the strings noticeably, then, holding the instrument between the knees, first grasp the bridge at the bottom with the thumb and forefinger of the right hand. You may then safely pull it back to it's normal position, which is slightly to the back rather than perpendicular.

♫

To clean the inside, warm a handful of dry barley grains; put this in through the f-holes of the instrument. Cover the f-holes with a cloth and shake the instrument in every direction for a while, then take off the cloth and shake out the barley, with the table held sloping down from the G side. The barley will carry with it all the dust, much of which will be attached to the grains by static electricity.

♫

Cleaning the outside is the operation which is more hazardous to the instrument, and the more delicate. Strictly speaking, one ought never perform this operation, in which the instrument always loses some part of its finish. The damage is not always immediately visible, but becomes gradually apparent with time, all the more reason when this degradation is repeated. Ideally, before cleaning varnish, one ought to know its composition.

Alcohol is disastrous to all the old Italian varnishes. One drop is enough to cause a permanent blemish.

Alkaline solutions (soda, potash), nearly always attack violin varnish of every period and nationality.

Generally instruments withstand a mixture of spirits of turpentine and linseed oil. Some specialists add a little alcohol to give it more bite. Others, less scrupulous, add finely powdered pumice stone.

Some amateurs clean their Cremonas with gasoline. Cremonese varnish is essentially undamaged by this product, but the process poses an problem. Gasoline leaves behind after evaporating, despite the most careful wiping, a thin oily coat which attracts dust. After a period of time the instrument again becomes just as dirty as before.

Others rub their instruments with linseed oil from time to time, intending to "feed" the varnish that has become, as they think, too dry over time. This practice has no sound basis and is in any case needless.

In keeping instruments perfectly clean, all these unsuitable things should be avoided.

———————

# THE VARIOUS PARTS OF A BOWED INSTRUMENT. NOMENCLATURE AND DEFINITIONS.

Figures 14, 15, 16, 17.

N.B. -- All measurements given are average.

### THE HEAD, Fig. 14 and 15.

The upper part on which the strings terminate for tightening. It includes:

**The Volute.** - The spiral that finishes the head.

**The Button(s).** - The small cylindrical projection that terminates the volute on the right and left.

**The Pegbox.** - Where the pegs are located.

**The *Coulisse*.** - Back of the pegbox.

**The *Nervure*.** - The longitudinal ridge dividing the coulisse into two equal, symmetrical parts.

**The Mortise.** - That part of the pegbox which is hollowed out to allow the strings to be attached to the pegs.

**The Cheeks.** - These two surfaces enclose the mortise on the right and left.

**The Chamfer.** - The bevel on the edge that goes around the coulisse and the volute as far as the button, as well as the bevel on the outside edge of the cheeks. Fig. 16.

**The Pegs.** - Pieces of wood (boxwood, ebony, or rosewood), drilled with a small hole and used to tighten the strings. Fig. 17.

### THE NECK, Fig. 14 and 15.

The narrow part between the head and body of the instrument. It is flat on the side nearer the table and rounded on the other. It includes:

**The Fingerboard.** - A piece of ebony, glued to the flat surface of the neck, beginning at the nut, over which the strings pass. Fig. 18.

Length:

| Violin | Viola | Cello | Bass |
|--------|-------|-------|------|
| 27 cm | 30 cm | 57 cm | 84 cm |

Fig. 18

**The Nut.** - A small piece of ebony, located at the upper end of the neck against the fingerboard. It is a little higher than

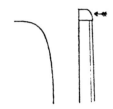

the latter and provided with four grooves which carry the strings on their way to the pegs. Fig. 19.

### THE TABLE OR SOUNDBOARD, Fig. 20.

The part located on top, that is, on the side nearest the fingerboard and the strings. Together with the back and the ribs, it forms the sound box or the *body*.

It is of spruce (picea), the grain lengthwise; of one, or usually, two pieces glued together.

Its greatest thickness is at the center. This decreases very gradually to the edges where it again increases.

Thickness at the post:

| Violin | Viola | Cello | Bass |
|--------|-------|-------|------|
| 3 mm | 4 mm | 5 mm | 9-10 mm |

The table includes:

**The Cheeks.** - Those parts located to the right and left, where the thickness is least:

| Violin | Viola | Cello | Bass |
|--------|-------|-------|------|
| 2 mm | 2.5 mm | 3 mm | 4.5 mm |

**The Edges.** - The part of the table over the ribs. Thickness:

| Violin | Viola | Cello | Bass |
|--------|-------|-------|------|
| 3 mm | 4 mm | 4 mm | 7 mm |

**The Sound Holes or F's** - Lengthwise openings in the shape of an *f*, placed symmetrically in the table. Note the *holes*, the *"nanny goats" (biques)* or *wings*, the *outside notches* and the *inside notches*. The imaginary line connecting these inside notches gives the exact location of the bridge. Fig. 21.

**The Saddle.** - A small piece of ebony glued at the very bottom of the table which supports the tailpiece fastener.

Figures 20, 21.

THE BACK, Fig. 22

The part located opposite to the table and parallel to it.

It is nearly always of maple, rarely of poplar, of one or two pieces.

Like the table it is thickest in the center. It decreases markedly toward the edges, where it again increases.

Thickness at the post:

| Violin | Viola | Cello | Bass |
|---|---|---|---|
| 4.5 mm | 4.5 mm | 8 mm | 12-20 mm |

Edge thickness, same as the table.

Minimum thicknesses:

| Violin | Viol | Cello | Bass |
|---|---|---|---|
| 1.7 mm | 2 mm | 3 mm | 5 mm |

**The Button.** - The small semicircular projection of the back

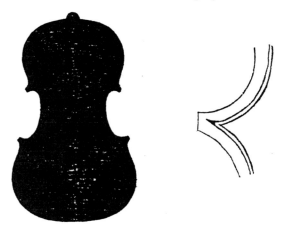

at the end of the neck, which provides support to it.

Figures 22, 23.

PARTS COMMON TO THE TABLE AND BACK

**The C's.** - The cutouts at the right and left of the body of the instrument that form, so to speak, the waist.

**The Corners.** - The four points located symmetrically at the top and bottom of the C's.

**The Purfling.** - The inlay made of three narrow strips of wood put together that frame the table and back a few mm from the edge. Fig. 23. For the

| Violin | Viola | Cello | Bass |
|---|---|---|---|
| 4 mm | 5 mm | 6 mm | 7 mm |

The width of the complete purfling is

| Violin | Viola | Cello | Bass |
|---|---|---|---|
| 1.5 mm | 1.5 mm | 2 mm | 2.5-3 mm |

**The Miter.** - The joining of the purfling in the corner. Fig. 23.

**The "beak" (bee sting).** - The small point shaped like a bird's beak at the very end of the miter. Fig. 23.

**The Channeling.** - The valley cut into the table and back over the purfling a small distance from the edge that is blended into the arching.

**The Arching.** - The shape of the table and back, concave on the inside and convex on the outside, obtained by hollowing out the inside and cutting away to form the surface.

Height of the arching:

| Violin | Viola | Cello | Bass |
|---|---|---|---|
| 13 mm | 15 mm | 22 mm | 40 mm |

**The Ribs.** - Strips of wood (maple) placed perpendicular to the table and back and connecting them, and bent with heat to fit the outlines. Fig. 24.

Height:

| Violin | Viola | Cello | Bass |
|---|---|---|---|
| 3 cm | 3.8-4 cm | 11-12 cm | 20 cm |

Thickness:

| Violin | Viola | Cello | Bass |
|---|---|---|---|
| 1 mm | 1.2 mm | 1.5 mm | 2 mm |

**The Blocks.** - Six pieces of wood glued inside the body to the ribs and of the same height. The four corner blocks are of a triangular shape, the upper and lower blocks are oblong, one side matching the shape of the ribs to which it is glued, the other smoothed into an oval shape. Plate III.

**The Linings.** - Small strips of light wood placed inside the body against the ribs matching their shape, bent with heat as the ribs were, and flush with their edges, which they are meant to reinforce. After they are in place they are trimmed with a bevel toward the inside. Following Stradivarius, the middle linings in the better instruments are let into the corner blocks. Fig. 25 and Plate III. [p. 27]

Thickness at the time of installation:

| Violin | Viola | Cello | Bass |
|---|---|---|---|
| 2 mm | 2.5 mm | 3 mm | 3.5 mm |

| Height: | | | |
|---|---|---|---|
| Violin | Viola | Cello | Bass |
| 7 mm | 9 mm | 1.2 cm | 1.8 cm |

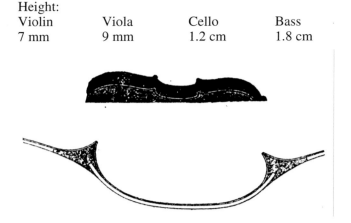

Figures 24, 25.

**The Bar.** - A piece of spruce cut on the quarter glued lengthwise inside the table and matching its shape. It is highest at the inside notches of the *f's* and decreases toward the two ends which are finished in a bevel. It is placed under the left foot of the bridge. Plate III. [p. 26]

Its dimensions:

| Violin | Viola | Cello | Bass |
|---|---|---|---|
| **Length:** | | | |
| 28 cm | 30 cm | 60 cm | 85 cm |
| **Thickness:** | | | |
| 5 mm | 6 mm | 9 to 10 mm | 2.5 cm |
| **Height of Maxima:** | | | |
| 1.1 cm | 1.5 cm | 2.3 cm | 3.5 to 4 cm |

**The Post.** - A spruce rod placed inside, vertically, between the table and the back. Fig. 2. [p. 15]

| Diameter: | | | |
|---|---|---|---|
| Violin | Viola | Cello | Bass |
| 6 mm | 8 mm | 12 mm | 20 mm |

(See chapter V.) [p. 17]

**The Bridge.** - A small piece of maple, placed vertically on the table, on an imaginary through the inside notches of the *f's*. Note the *four grooves* on the top edge, which carry the strings, the *two feet*, and the decorative opening in the middle, called the *heart*.

Fig. 26, violin. Fig. 27, cello.

| Height: | | | |
|---|---|---|---|
| Violin | Viola | Cello | Bass |
| 3.2 cm | 3.5 cm | 9.5 cm | 15 cm |

(For the other Measurements see chapter IV.) [p. 15]

**The Button.** - A peg of ebony, boxwood, or rosewood deeply embedded into the lower ribs and block. Its head projects to provide a solid point of support for the tailpiece. Fig. 28.

**The Endpin.** - A movable wooden rod, with a steel point at its end, mounted in the "button" of the cello. It supports the cello on the floor and keeps it at a convenient height without tiring. Fig. 29, 30.

Figures 28, 29, 30

**The Chinrest** (for the Violin and Viola). - A plate of wood or plastic of various shapes, mounted left of the tail gut over the table in various ways to support the chin at a height suitable for the build of the player. Figures 31, 32, 33.

Fig. 31, 32, 33

**The Mute.** - A small piece of ebony, metal, or horn placed when desired on the bridge to *mute* the sound and to effect a particular *timbre*. Figures 34, 35.

**The Tailpiece.** - Also called the *string-holder*, usually of ebony. It has a tie at one end for the button; at the other four holes to accept the strings. Fig. 36.

Figures 34, 35, 36.

**The Strings.** - These are made from the small intestine of the sheep. The G of the violin, the G and C of the cello and the viola are overwound with thin metal wire. (See chapter II.)

**The Varnish.** - The outside coating intended to give the instrument its tonal quality and to protect it from environmental disturbances. It may be of four kinds: spirit, essential oil, oil, or mixed, that is, a combination of two of these kinds, essential oil and oil.

## PRINCIPAL TERMS USED IN VIOLIN MAKING

**Enlargement.** - An operation to increase the dimensions of an instrument.

**Wood Cut on the Slab.** - Wood cut with surfaces parallel to the length of the trunk. (Cut along the rings.) Fig. 37.

**Wood Cut on the Quarter.** - Wood cut lengthwise of the trunk into billets in the shape of triangular prisms whose apexes meet at the center. (Cut along the radii.) Fig. 38.

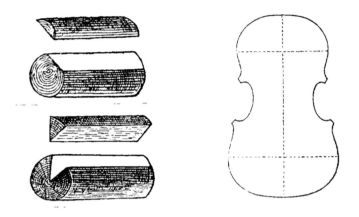

Figures 37, 38, 39.

**Rosin.** - A solid mixture of resinous products and by products meant to give bite to the bow hair.

**Opening.** - The process of removing the table. - This operation is usually done with a dull knife.

**The Stop.** - In practice, the ratio of the line from the nut to the edge of the table, on the one hand, and on the other, that which separates the edge of the table from the imaginary line through the inside notches of the *f*'s. Fig. 1. (To calculate the stop, see chapter III.)

**Dimensions.** - First, the length of the table or back (less the button); second, the maximum upper and lower widths of the table or back. Fig. 39.

| | Violin | Viola | Cello | Bass |
|---|---|---|---|---|
| Length: | 35.5 cm | 41 cm | 75.5 cm | 1.5 m |
| Upper Width: | 17 cm | 19 cm | 35 cm | 54 cm |
| Lower Width: | 21 cm | 23.2 cm | 44 cm | 70 cm |

**Doubling.** - A piece of wood glued to the inside under a crack or where it has become too thin.

**To Double.** - To install a doubling.

**With the Grain.** - Refers to a piece of wood split or cut parallel to the grain.

**Setting the Neck.** - The process whereby the neck is fitted and glued into the mortise cut for it.

**Grafting.** - The process of fitting the old head onto a new neck.

**To Purfle.** - The process of inlaying the purfling.

**Supplies.** - Material for the instrument parts list.

**Setting Up, Taking Down.** - The process of installing or removing the replaceable parts (strings, bridge, pegs, etc.)

**Graduating.** - The process of giving the table and back their "rational" thicknesses.

**Cutting Down.** - An operation to reduce the size of an instrument that is considered to be too large.

**Projection of the Neck.** - The proper position of the neck to give the fingerboard its correct slope and to set the angle that the strings make over the bridge. (See chapter IV.)

**Restoration of the Arching.** - The process of renewing the original curvature in distorted arching.

**Closing.** - The process of gluing the table back on.

**Cleats.** - Little rectangles of wood trimmed into pyramids, about 5 mm by 5 mm on a side, intended to reinforce joints or cracks on the inside. Plate IV.

THE BOW, Plate I. [see page 12]

**Its total weight:**

| Violin | Viola | Cello | Bass |
|---|---|---|---|
| 55-60 g | 60-65 g | 70-75 g | 135-150 g |

**Its length, including the button:**

| Violin | Viola | Cello | Bass |
|---|---|---|---|
| 74-74 cm | 74-75 cm | 72-73 cm | 68-70 cm |

**The Stick.** - Generally of Pernambuco wood, cut with the grain, then sawn in a gradual curve, and finally bent with heat.

**Its diameter:**

| | Violin | Viola | Cello |
|---|---|---|---|
| At the head: | 5 mm | 5.5 mm | 12 mm |
| In the middle: | 8 mm | 8.5 mm | 9 mm |
| At the foot: | 8.5 mm | 9 mm | 10 mm |

**The Head.** - The upper part of the stick where the hair is fixed in the mortise cut for this purpose.
It is finished here with an ivory plate glued over a thin plate of ebony.

| Width: | Violin | Viola | Cello |
|---|---|---|---|
| | 10 mm | 10.5 mm | 12 mm |

**The Hair.** - A hank of white horsehair for the violin, viola, and cello, and of black hair for the bass; leaving the head it is stretched by means of the frog located at the mortise in the lower part of the stick.

Number of hairs in the hank:

| Violin | Viola | Cello | Bass |
|---|---|---|---|
| 120-130 | 150-190 | 210-225 | 210 to 225 |

**The Frog.** - Usually of ebony, sometimes of ivory or tortoise shell. It moves back and forth by means of a screw operated by the button at the end of the stick, thus tightening or loosening the hair according to the requirements of performance. Note in particular the channel (*coulisse*) for the stick, the *slide*, a small plate of ebony veneered with pearl serving to cover the hair, the *ferrule* or *passant*.

**The Fittings.** [wrapping and grip] - A course of silver wound around the stick, near the frog, over a length of 10 cm, also a small band of leather glued around the stick, right next to the frog, to afford a grip for the fingers.

———————

## WORKS ON VIOLIN MAKING WORTH CONSULTING

**Heron-Allen, E.** - *De Fidiculis Bibliographia.* Being an attempt toward a bibliography of the violin and all other instr. played with a bow in ancient and modern times. 2 vol. in 12 installments,
London, 1890-1894.

- *Violin-making* as It Was and Is; being a historical, practical and theoretical treatise on the "Science and Art of Violin-making" for the use of violin makers and players, upwards of 200 illustrations. 2$^d$ edition. London, 1884.

**Appian Bennewitz, P. O.** - *Die Geige, der Geigenbau und die Bogensverfertigung.* Eine auf Grund der Theorie und Geschichte der Bogeninstrumente, sowie des hervorragensten Meistern des Geigenbaues beobachteten Verfahrens gegebene Anweisung zur Herstellung der verschieden Geigen und ihres Zubehörs, eingeleitet durch Eine Darstellung der darauf bezüglichen Lehren der Physik. Mit einem Atlas enthaltend 14 Foliotafeln und 56 in Text gedruckten Abbildungen. Gr. 8°, Weimar.

**Bagatella, A.** - *Regolae per la costruzione dei violini e violoncelli e violoni.* Memoria presentata all Accademia di scienze, lettere e arti di Padova al Concorso del premio dell'arti del, 1782, e coronata dalla stesse Accademia, 1786.

**Boulee, Ch.** - *Leopold Widhalm, luthier allemand.* S. I. M. Revue musicale publiée par la Société internationale (Section de Paris), n° 7 (15 juillet 1910)

**Balfour, B. and Co.** - *How to Tell the Nationality of Old Violins.* Being a practical guide to the simple distinguishing points found in English, French, Dutch, and Italian violins. Illustrated. London, Balfour and Co. 1900.

Catalogue du musée du Conservatoire national de musique de Paris, par Gustave Chouquet.

1$^{er}$ supplément, par Leon Pillaut.
2$^e$ " "
3$^e$ " "

**Catalogue descriptif et analytique de Musée du Conservatoire royal de musique de Bruxelles**, par Victor-Charles Mahillon.

1er volume. Nos 1 à 576.
2e " " 577 à 1321.
3e " " 1322 à 2055.

**Coutagne, Henry.** - *Gaspard Duiffoproucart et les luthiers lyonnais du XVI$^e$ siecle.* Paris, 1893.

**De Piccolelis, Giovanni.** - *Liutai antichi e moderni.* Note criticobiografiche. Florence, 1885.

- *Liutai antichi e moderni.* Genealogia degli Amati e dei Guarneri secondo i documenti ultimamente ritrovati negli atti e stati d'anime delle antiche Parrocchie di S. Faustino e di S. Donato di Cremona. Note aggiunte alla I$^a$ edizione. Firenze, 1886.

**Drogemeyer Herm. Aug.** - *Die Geige.* Mit eingehender Belehrung über den internationalen unlauteren Wettbewerb auf dem Gebiete des Geigenbaues und Geigenhandels. 3$^e$ édit. Berlin, 1903.

**Engel, Carl.** - *Researches into the early history of the Violin Family,* 2é edit. 1874.

- *Cat. of the Spec. Exhit. of ancient Mus. instr.,* 1872.

**Fetis F.-J.** - *Antoine Stradivari, luthier celebre, connu sous Le nom de Stradivarius,* précédé de recherches historiques et critiques sur l'origine et les transformations des instruments à archet, et suivi d'analyses théoriques sur l'archet, et sur Francois Tourte, auteur de ces derniers perfectionnements. Paris, 1856.

**Gallay, J.** - *Les luthiers italiens aux XVII$^e$ et XVIII$^e$ siècles.* Nouvelle edition du *Parfait luthier,* de l'abbe Sibire, suivie de notes sur les maîtres des diverses écoles. Paris, 1869.

**Greilsamer, Lucien.** - *Le Vernis de Crémone.* Étude historique et critique. Paris, 1908.

**Grillet, Laurent.** - *Les ancêtres du violon et du Violoncelle, les luthiers et les fabricants d'archets.* 2 vol. Paris, 1901.

**Hart, George.** - *Le violon, les luthiers célèbres et leurs imitateurs,* contenant de nombreuses gravures sur bois d'apres les photographies des violons de Stardivarius, Guarnerius, Amati, etc. Traduit de l'anglais, par A. Royer. Paris, 1886.

**Hill, W. Henry, Arthur F. Hill and Alfred E. Hill.**
- *Antonio Stradivari, his Life and Work* (1644-1737), with an introductory note by lady Huggins. Drawings by Shirley Slocombe, chromolithographed by Nister of Nuremberg. London, 1902.

**Hill and sons.** - *The Salabue Stradivari.* A history and critical description of the famous violin commonly called *Le Messie.* London, 1891.

- *The Tuscan Stradivari.* A short account of a violin made by Stradivari for Cosimo de Medici, grand Duke of Tuscany in 1690.

- *The Life and Work of Maggini.*

**Jacquot, E.** - *Les Medard, luthiers lorrains.* Paris, 1896.

**Lütgendorff, Willilbald Leo, Freiherr von.** - *Die Geigen und Lautenmacher vom Mittelalter bis zur Gegenwart.* Frankfurt-am Main, 1904.

**Mailand, Eug.** - Découverte des anciens Vernis italiens employés pour les instruments a cordes et à archet. Paris, 1859.

**Maugin et Maigne.** - *Nouveau Manuel complet du luthier.* Paris, Roret, nouvelle édit. 1894.

**Mordret, Léon.** - *La Lutherie artistique.* Paris, 1885.

- Les Violons de Crémone. Rouen, 1898.

**Otto Jakob Aug.** - *Über den Bau der Bogeninstrumente und über die Arbeiten der vorzüglichsten Instrumentenmacher.* Jena, 1828. 2ᵉ édit., Jena, 1873.

**Pierre, Constant.** - *Les Facteurs d'instruments de musique, les luthiers et la facture instrumentale.* Paris, 1893.

**Reade, Ch.** - *Readiana.* Leipzig, Tauchnitz, édit. Vol. 2, 1909.

**Rinaldi Ben. Gioff.** - *Classica fabbricazione di volini in Piemonte.* Turin, 1873.

**Ruf Seb.** - *Jacob Stainer.* 2ᵉ édit. Innsbruck, 1892.

**Savart, F.** - *Mémoire sur la construction des instruments à cordes et à archet.* Paris, 1818.

**Schebek, E.** - *Der Geigenbau in Italien, und sein deutscher Ursprung.* Prague, 1874.

**Sibire, l'Abbé Antoine.** - *La Chelonomie ou le parfait luthier.* Paris, 1806.

**Tolbecque, A.** - *L'Art du luthier.* Niort, 1903.

**Vidal Antoine.** - *La Lutherie et les luthiers.* Paris, 1889.

- *Les Instruments à archet,* orné de planches gravées à l'eau-forte, par Frédéric Hillemacher. Paris, 1875 à 1878. 3 volumes.

**Wasiliewski, W.-J.-V.** - *Die Violine und ihre Meister.* Leipzig, 1869.
- *Die Violine im 16. Jahrhundert.*
- *Das Violoncell und seine Geschichte.*

**Wit, P. de.** - *Geigenzettel alter Meister.* Leipzig, 1901.

**Youssupoff, Nicolaï, Prince de.** - *Luthomonographie historique raisonnée.* Munich, 1856.

**Zamminer, F.** - *Die Musik und die musikalischen Instrumente in ihrer Beziehung zu den Gesetzen der Akustik.* Giessen, 1855.

———

**[Greilsamer, Lucien —** Alsatian writer (Musicographe Alsacien), author of very interesting works on violin making:

1.) *The Anatomy and Physiology of the Violin, Viola, and Cello, New Looks at the Varnish of Cremona.* Paris, Delagrave (latest edition 1924), 238 pages.

2.) *The Health of the Violin, the Viola and Cello.* S.I.M. 1908, published the same year in Paris by Delagrave (latest edition 1924), 121 pages.

3.) *The Forerunners of the Violin.* S.I.M. April 1911, pages 58-62.

4.) *The Making of Bowed Instruments,* in the Encyclopedia of Music (2nd part, vol.2, pages 1708-1752).

(This reference is translated from Vannes, *Dictionnaire Universel des Luthiers,* page 137.)]

# The Poor Fiddler's Ode to his Old Fiddle.

Torn,
Worn,
Oppressed I mourn
B a d,
S a d,
Three-quarters mad :
Money gone,
Credit none,
Duns at door,
Half a score,
Wife in lain,
Twins again,
Others ailing,
Nurse a railing,
Billy hooping,
Betsy crouping,
Besides poor Joe,
With festered toe.
Come, then, my fiddle,
Come, my time-worn friend,
With  gay  and  brilliant  sounds,
Some  sweet, tho'  transient  solace lend.
Thy  polished  neck,  in  close  embrace,
I  clasp,  whilst  joy  illumes  my  face
When  o'er  thy  strings  I  draw  my  bow,
My  drooping  spirit  pants  to  rise :
A  lively  strain  I  touch — and,  lo !
I  seem  to  mount  above  the  skies.
There,  on  Fancy's  wing  I  soar,
Heedless  of  the  duns  at  door ;
Oblivious  all,  I  feel  my  woes  no more ;
But  skip  o'er  the  strings,
As  my  old  Fiddle  sings,
"Cheerily, oh ! merrily go !
" Presto !  good  master,
" You  very  well  know,
" I  will  find  Music,
" If  you  will  find  bow,
" From E,  up  in alto, to  G,  down below."
Fatigued,  I  pause,  to  change  the  time
For  some  *Adagio*,  solemn  and  sublime.
With  graceful  action  moves  the  sinuous  arm ;
My  heart,  responsive  to  the  soothing  charm,
Throbs  equably ;  whilst  every  health-corroding  care
Lies  prostrate,  vanquished  by  the  soft  mellifluous  air.
More and more plaintive grown, my eyes with tears o'erflow,
And  resignation  mild,  soon  smooths  my  wrinkled  brow.
*Reedy* Hautboy may squeak, wailing Flauto may squall,
The  Serpent  may  grunt,  and  the  Trombone  may  bawl,
But  my  Poll,* my  old  Fiddle's  the  Prince  of  them  all.
Could  e'en  Dryden  return,  thy  praise  to  rehearse,
His  Ode  to  Cecilia  would  seem  rugged  verse.
Now  to  thy  *case*,  in  flannel  warm  to  lie
Till call'd again to pipe thy master's eye.
\* Apollo.

FROM THE "MUSICAL WORLD," OF AUGUST 5. 1841, WITH PERMISSION.
——————————————————————————————EDITOR.